A fine book on biblical preaching fro
Jonathan Lamb is well known for hi
expositions of Scripture, and this bo
spirituality, vision and practice whic.
Peppered with illustrations, worked examples and practical tools,
Preaching Matters will challenge and help preachers and
congregations alike.
*John Risbridger, Chair of Keswick Ministries, and Minister and Team
Leader of Above Bar Church, Southampton*

Jonathan Lamb has been a pioneer in training expository
preaching movements in many countries around the world,
including Latin America, and we are delighted that he is now
sharing his experience with us. Through Nehemiah and Ezra's
journey, Jonathan shows us the essential elements of biblical
preaching. I was very encouraged to see that he has included
'praying the Word' as an important part of preparation.
*Igor Améstegui, formerly the General Secretary of the Bolivian IFES
movement, and now the coordinator for Langham Preaching in Latin
America*

This is a refreshing, clear, helpful and accessible book which is
the fruit of many years of faithful preaching and patient training
of preachers. I particularly enjoyed the final section on the
two-way dynamic with those who hear, and are shaped by,
faithful expository preaching.
*Christopher Ash, Director of the Proclamation Trust's Cornhill
Training Course*

Like many sporting heroes, some of the best preachers perform
well, but are unable to coach others to be better. Jonathan Lamb,
however, is a rare combination: an exceptional preacher, a clear
writer and an excellent coach. That's what makes *Preaching
Matters* such a treat: biblical, accessible, practical and quotable!
Sell your shirt, extend the mortgage if necessary, but buy, read,
mark and learn from this superb guide on the hows, whys and
wherefores of preaching.
Dr Steve Brady, Principal of Moorlands College, Christchurch, UK

At last, a book on preaching for both preachers and listeners. If you're a preacher, *Preaching Matters* will show you how to preach without resorting to gimmicks and instead rely on the power of God's Word and Spirit. If you're a listener (and all of us are), it will show you how to listen to God's glory and to your benefit. Here is a fitting manifesto not just for the Keswick Convention, but for every local church.
Tim Chester, The Porterbrook Network

This biblical and practical book is very timely because preaching really does matter! New preachers will find it an essential guide to laying good foundations for a lifetime of preaching. 'Old hands' will benefit enormously from this refreshing exploration of the preaching ministry.
Stephen Gaukroger, author and Bible teacher, founder and Director of Clarion Trust International

As someone who rarely preaches, I wasn't sure how helpful I would find this book. But it didn't take me long before I realized the treasures it contained. Yes, it is great for the person setting out on a preaching ministry (actually, even if you have been preaching for many years this is brilliant revision!). What particularly struck me was that the insights and guidance aimed at preachers for understanding and applying God's Word are also so valuable for those leading Bible studies, involved in one-to-one work and even for individuals just wanting to understand God's Word better.
Revd Clare Hendry, Assistant Minister, Grace Church, Muswell Hill, London, and Assistant Tutor in Pastoral Theology at Wycliffe Hall, Oxford

When I heard that Jonathan Lamb had written a book on preaching, I thought, 'Who else would be in a better position to do so with universal appeal?' Jonathan Lamb has not only preached most of his life, but he has also observed and taught preaching on all the continents on this planet. Reading this book, I sense that here now is the distillation of his experience, observation and teaching. Do not be deceived by this book's simplicity of language. Take its instructions to heart, and you will soon be a person sent from God to your hearers.

Dr Conrad Mbewe, Pastor of Kabwata Baptist Church, and Chancellor of the African Christian University in Lusaka, Zambia

A direct, readable and wonderfully comprehensive book. Jonathan Lamb is not only himself a very gifted preacher, but has read widely into the subject and ornaments his teaching with apt quotations. I would think that he was writing mainly for those in the earlier days of preaching, but, speaking as one who has put in many miles along that particular road, I was personally helped on every page and found Jonathan Lamb's book a potent and salutary recall to first principles and basic essentials. I can't think of any aspect of the preacher or of the preacher's task left untouched (or unornamented). He is constantly insistent on application, whether we preachers are in our studies, in the pulpit, pastorally engaged with those to whom we preach, or summoned ourselves to Christlike living as the context and required foundation of our spoken word. No reader can fail to be driven more deeply into the Word of God as the preacher's source book and endless preoccupation, or to be renewed in determination to preach Jesus Christ as Lord. I feel personally very indebted to this book.

Alec Motyer, author and Bible expositor

In our Western culture that no longer believes in truth in any absolute sense, the role of preaching is more important than ever. As Christ works to transform the world, it is imperative that the faithful (both preachers and the laity) regain a deep confidence in the power of God's Word and Spirit. Jonathan Lamb reminds us of the power of God's Word to transform lives and the culture around us. He writes from his tremendous wealth of experience in pulpit ministry and training. I couldn't recommend this book more highly.

Rebecca Manley Pippert, author, evangelist, speaker

Like many, I like to highlight important and memorable points in a book. My copy of *Preaching Matters* is full of highlights! I

wish I could put this book, especially the foundational first three chapters, into the hands of every preacher. Preaching is simply too important to get wrong or do badly, and so *Preaching Matters* is rightly uncompromising in its assertion: 'The only true form of preaching is biblical preaching.' Amen! Forceful, true convictions married with godly practical advice make this one of the best books available on preaching.
Michael Raiter, Director of the Centre for Biblical Preaching, Melbourne, Australia

Jonathan Lamb's warm and inspiring summary of the important underlying dynamics of preaching will remind you – as it did me – of what really matters in preaching. Richly biblical, clearly written, flowing from a life of pulpit ministry and ministry to others who preach, this volume deserves to be read. I hope that many – preachers and listeners to preaching alike – will take its insights to heart. When they do so, preaching will accomplish more of what God designed it to do.
Revd Dr Greg Scharf, Professor of Pastoral Theology at Trinity Evangelical Divinity School, Deerfield, Illinois, and author of Prepared to Preach *and* Relational Preaching, *and, with John Stott,* The Challenge of Preaching

PREACHING
MATTERS

JONATHAN LAMB

PREACHING MATTERS

Encountering the Living God

INTER-VARSITY PRESS
Norton Street, Nottingham NG7 3HR, England
Email: ivp@ivpbooks.com
Website: www.ivpbooks.com

First published 2014

British Library Cataloguing in Publication Data
A catalogue record for this book is available from the British Library.

ISBN: 978-1-78359-149-7

Set in Dante 12/15pt
Typeset in Great Britain by CRB Associates, Potterhanworth, Lincolnshire
Printed and bound in Great Britain by 4edge Ltd, Hockley, Essex

*Inter-Varsity Press publishes Christian books that are true to the Bible and that
communicate the gospel, develop discipleship and strengthen the church for its
mission in the world.*

*Inter-Varsity Press is closely linked with the Universities and Colleges Christian
Fellowship, a student movement connecting Christian Unions in universities and
colleges throughout Great Britain, and a member movement of the International
Fellowship of Evangelical Students. Website: www.uccf.org.uk*

*To the courageous preachers of the Majority World
from whom I have gained so much inspiration*

Contents

Acknowledgments

Forty years ago this year, I heard a preacher at the British Keswick Convention speak about the urgency of mission, and I trace my call to full-time Christian service back to that sermon. Subsequently, it has been a privilege for me to have served with Keswick Ministries for many years, both in the UK and elsewhere, and I am grateful to the Council of the UK Keswick – and especially to the Chair of the Literature Committee, Elizabeth McQuoid – for the invitation to contribute to the Keswick Foundations Series. I am also indebted to the thousands of preachers around the world with whom I have enjoyed fellowship in the work of Langham Preaching, establishing indigenous preaching movements in their countries in order to encourage and equip a new generation of Bible preachers. I have been inspired by their courageous commitment to the gospel, their wholehearted commitment to the Word of God and their sacrificial commitment to their churches. I dedicate this small book to them. I am grateful for the constant generosity of my wife, Margaret, who continues to work tirelessly in support of our shared Christian service, and I must also express special thanks to Catherine Nicholson for her careful proofreading of the biblical texts, and to Eleanor Trotter of IVP for her sustained encouragement.

Preface

*Our prayer was for deep, clear, powerful teaching,
which would take hold of the souls of the people,
and overwhelm them, and lead them to a full, definite
and all-conquering faith in Jesus.*

This simple but profound prayer, expressed by Thomas Harford-Battersby as he reported on the 1880 Keswick Convention, explains why hundreds of thousands of Christians the world over have been committed to the Keswick movement. The *purpose* is nothing other than to see believers more whole-heartedly committed to Jesus Christ in every area of life, and the *means* the faithful, clear and relevant exposition of God's Word. All around the world, the Keswick movement has this purpose and this means. Whether it is to encourage discipleship, to call for holiness, to urge for mission, to appeal for unity, to provoke for life-change, to long for the Spirit, expounding the Bible is central to fulfilling these priorities.

Battersby was speaking at the end of the nineteenth century, but as I have travelled to different continents over recent years, I have frequently met Christians in various spheres of service whose lives have been impacted through meeting Christ in the preached Word, whether at Keswick (and there are many) or in their home congregations. I recall a conversation with a thoughtful physiotherapy student newly arrived at college who, on hearing a sermon on new life in

Christ from 2 Corinthians 5:17, was moved from a merely nominal Christianity to an all-conquering faith in Christ which changed his life and his future forever. Or a middle-aged married couple, bravely confronting the terminal illness of the wife, discovering that Jesus was all they needed, through the exposition of Habakkuk's closing doxology. Or some confident and successful professionals now serving God in Thailand, shaken from their complacency by the call of Christ in the Gospels. Or me, the author, burdened by some of the unexpected sorrows of Christian service, finding the comfort of Christ himself in the preaching of Isaiah's Servant Songs. Preaching matters, because it is a God-ordained means of encountering Christ.

Keswick Foundations is a series of books which tackle priority themes that have shaped the Keswick movement, themes which we believe are essential for the church. Given the central place of biblical preaching within the Keswick movement, an introductory title on the essentials of preaching seems especially appropriate, since all of our activities and ministry, for all age groups and all abilities, are built upon the foundation of God's Word. Beginning with an understanding and proclamation of the Bible, it is our prayerful intention for that truth to be lived and for believers to understand, but also to experience, the transforming power of the Word of the Lord.

This contribution to Keswick Foundations arose originally from a Keswick lecture delivered at the English Convention in 2010.[1] It seeks to address the core foundations for preaching, built around the dramatic story recounted in Nehemiah's memoirs. Whilst it offers some simple insights for preachers, it is not intended to be a detailed homiletics book, but an introduction to the dynamics that shape the task of biblical preaching, hopefully of use to speaker and listener alike. Since one of its three main sections relates to the congregation, and the importance of the listener's engagement as the Word is preached, our hope is that it will be read by church leaders and members alike who share the conviction that preaching matters, and that spiritual life and renewal at all levels will come only through the Spirit-empowered proclamation of the Word of God.

We are also aware that much explanation of the Bible is done outside of the pulpit – in home groups, youth events, one-to-one Bible studies, women's meetings and in many other contexts. So, whether you are a speaker or a listener, a preacher or a group leader, we hope that that this simple introduction to the dynamics of preaching will strengthen your confidence in that ministry, and help you experience that Word in such a way that you are led to a 'full, definite and all-conquering faith in Jesus'.

Jonathan Lamb
Oxford, UK

Introduction

One of the oldest Bible translations in the English language is the King James Bible. A few years ago, its 400th anniversary was celebrated, with the media carrying various reports of how people viewed the impact of this remarkable translation. Here is what one of many celebrities said: 'You can't appreciate English literature unless you are to some extent steeped in the King James Bible. Not to know the King James Bible is to be, in some small way, a barbarian.'

Believe it or not, these supportive words came from the notorious atheist Professor Richard Dawkins. And there were many similar words of adulation. Most tended to highlight the influence of the KJV on language and culture. Joan Bakewell declared the King James Version to be 'one of the greatest works of literature ever written'. And whilst these statements were indeed true, it made me wonder what Moses or Jeremiah or Paul would have said in response to such praise. Someone once suggested that it would be rather like picking up the original manuscript of Einstein's *Theory of Relativity* and saying, 'What beautiful handwriting!', as if that were the highest praise that could be offered.

There is, of course, much more to God's Word than its literary legacy, remarkable though that is. Some years ago, a man called J. B. Phillips was working on a paraphrase of the Bible and explained that the experience was similar to working on the mains electricity of a house, but doing so with the electricity still switched on. It was an extraordinary experience – the book was 'live'; it was powerful and energizing. As Martin Luther put it, 'The Bible is alive – it has hands and grabs hold of me; it has feet and runs after me.'

The Bible is full of dynamic descriptions of itself. Jeremiah said that God's Word was like fire in his bones or like a hammer that breaks a rock in pieces (Jeremiah 20:9; 23:29). Paul described it as the sword of the Spirit (Ephesians 6:17). The idea is repeated in Hebrews 4: 'alive and active. Sharper than any double-edged sword' (verse 12). Jesus said that the Word was the seed which produced a wonderful harvest. And there is the intriguing story in Luke 24 of two disciples walking home to Emmaus after the dramatic events of Jesus' crucifixion in Jerusalem. They didn't recognize Jesus, but he deliberately chose not to reveal himself, other than through the Bible: 'And beginning with Moses and all the Prophets, he explained to them what was said in all the Scriptures concerning himself.' Their response? 'Were not our hearts burning within us while he talked with us on the road and opened the Scriptures to us?' (verse 32).

In other words, it was through Scripture that they encountered the living Christ. This is the reason why our churches are committed to listening to, understanding and explaining God's Word, and why the Keswick movement continues to be focused on Scripture. We believe God's Word has the same dynamic impact today. *Preaching matters*. When the Bible is faithfully and relevantly explained, it transforms understandings and attitudes, it challenges and reshapes worldviews and, most of all, it draws us into a living relationship with God through Christ.

I remember a friend of mine who, struggling with the challenges of bringing up a child who had severe learning difficulties, found her Christian faith less and less relevant. Could she *really* trust God? Were the calls to live with hope merely sentimental expressions born of wishful thinking? Yet, over several Sundays, listening to the story of Ruth being preached with pastoral relevance, she told me that this ancient story had, by God's grace, transformed her perspective on her family situation and restored her trust in God's good purposes. This is happening all the time and all around the world today.

The Bible and preaching

It is this conviction which lies behind all biblical preaching, and it is for this reason that the Bible itself, early Christian history, the story of revivals, the shaping of societies and the transformation of individuals all bear witness to the fact that *preaching is effective only when the Bible is at the centre.*

But I can hear someone say, 'Surely every preacher preaches from the Bible – why write about the obvious?' This is certainly a legitimate question. The preacher in any congregation, any tradition, any country, presumably sees their task as explaining the Bible. We know the force of the New Testament commands to 'preach the Word' and, when we gather for a church service, we assume that after the Bible passage has been read, the preacher stands before the congregation, Bible open, with the intention of proclaiming the Word of the Lord. Surely every preacher does that?

Sadly not. I spoke recently to a pastor who said that, in his country, pastors and preachers write their sermon and then look for a Bible passage to illustrate it. Wherever I tell this story, I hear embarrassed laughter – that pastor is surely not alone. Too often, the Bible doesn't set the agenda; it is simply the background music. In many countries, topical preaching – often very loosely based on a string of Bible references – is the main type. The danger is that such preaching does not allow the Bible to do the talking, but can easily substitute the power of that Word with anecdotes threaded together around a thin popular theme. Indeed, there is an epidemic of what we might call 'preaching-lite'. Such preaching has no transforming power, for it is drained of biblical authority. I've often spoken with friends who, having heard a lively conference speaker, describe the entertaining and dramatic stories, but bemoan the fact that they have not heard the Word of the Lord. Memorable and compelling stories are vital in preaching, but if the Word of God in Scripture is concealed or marginalized or ignored, then nothing will change and nothing will last.

Too often, the Bible doesn't set the agenda; it is simply the background music.

So, here is the key proposition: the only true form of preaching is biblical preaching. And by biblical preaching, we mean preaching that places the Bible at the centre, exposing the Bible's force and power. In almost all situations, I would even want to go a step further: biblical preaching is preaching that expounds a Bible passage. Of course, there is an important place within the church's diet for thematic or topical preaching, but this too is usually best developed through the careful explanation of a main passage, supplemented by other biblical material. This book aims to present the case for preaching from a Bible passage as the primary and most effective way of declaring God's Word.

Preaching and spiritual growth

So, preaching with the Bible at the centre is critically important. Many years ago, Jim Packer, speaking on the importance of the Bible, introduced his sermon by talking about the redwoods in northern California. These magnificent trees are carefully fenced off, the reason being that, although they are enormous, they have a very shallow root system, so, as more and more visitors march round them, the soil is loosened around the roots and they become very vulnerable. In fact, it wouldn't take too much wind to topple them. Packer commented that, although there have been many signs of growth in the evangelical church, there is also an unmistakable shallowness. And the primary focal point, he suggested, was uncertainty and confusion with regard to the nature and use of the Bible. Sadly, if there is uncertainty here, you must expect uncertainty everywhere else. It is a startling paradox that, at the very time when the Bible is most freely available in so many versions and formats, it is also effectively silent in so many areas of church life.

There is less commitment to personal Bible reading, less time devoted to the reading of Scripture in homes and church services, and even a marginalization of the Bible in preaching. All of this inevitably has serious consequences. If churches are to stand firm against wind and tide, if Christian disciples are to become mature in the faith, then their roots must be deeply nourished by God's Word. As Jim Packer once expressed it: 'The church must live by God's Word as its necessary food and steer by that Word as its guiding star. Without preaching it is not conceivable that this will be either seen or done.'[1] So, the main task in pastoral ministry is to ensure that the ministry of the Word (which includes, but is far more than, preaching) is the heartbeat of the church's life and work.

Preaching and the congregation

One of the convictions behind this book, therefore, is that preaching is a community event which requires the active participation of the congregation. It matters for all of us, since it is the way that the church as a community encounters the living God. We need to find ways to integrate the preached Word in our worship, as well as make that Word central to our small-group ministry, use that Word in pastoral counselling, proclaim that Word in evangelism, and live that Word by example in our life and family. In several chapters of this book, I deliberately focus on the engagement of the congregation, including the need to ensure the Word's centrality in chapter 1, the call to pray and study Scripture in chapters 2 and 3, the importance of its application in chapters 6, 7 and 9, and – most particularly – the various ways by which congregations can play their part in preaching, outlined in chapter 8.

We will look at several themes that emerge from one dramatic story, where God's Word had a dynamic impact on his people at a critical moment in their history. This story is recorded in Nehemiah's memoirs, and we will focus our gaze on Nehemiah 8:1–12. Using that as the primary passage, the structure of this book will follow three primary dynamic elements:

The Word of God and the heart of preaching
The teacher and the work of preaching
The congregation and the purpose of preaching

We will explore each of these themes through the experience of God's people in Jerusalem, when Ezra the teacher led them to a life-transforming encounter with the living God.

Please have Nehemiah 8:1–12 open in your Bible, on your phone, or by using a bookmark, as you work through the following chapters. And first, as you read the Bible passage, ask yourself the question: What are the elements in this story that demonstrate what happens when the Bible is opened up as it ought to be?

Nehemiah 8:1–12 (NIV)

When the seventh month came and the Israelites had settled in their towns, all the people came together as one in the square before the Water Gate. They told Ezra the teacher of the Law to bring out the Book of the Law of Moses, which the LORD had commanded for Israel.

So on the first day of the seventh month Ezra the priest brought the Law before the assembly, which was made up of men and women and all who were able to understand. He read it aloud from daybreak till noon as he faced the square before the Water Gate in the presence of the men, women and others who could understand. And all the people listened attentively to the Book of the Law.

Ezra the teacher of the Law stood on a high wooden platform built for the occasion. Beside him on his right stood Mattithiah, Shema, Anaiah, Uriah, Hilkiah and Maaseiah; and on his left were Pedaiah, Mishael, Malkijah, Hashum, Hashbaddanah, Zechariah and Meshullam.

Ezra opened the book. All the people could see him because he was standing above them; and as he opened it, the people all stood up. Ezra praised the LORD, the great God; and all the people lifted their hands and responded, 'Amen! Amen!' Then they bowed down and worshipped the LORD with their faces to the ground.

The Levites – Jeshua, Bani, Sherebiah, Jamin, Akkub, Shabbethai, Hodiah, Maaseiah, Kelita, Azariah, Jozabad, Hanan and Pelaiah – instructed the people in the Law while the people were standing there. They read from the Book of the Law of God, making it clear and giving the meaning so that the people understood what was being read.

Then Nehemiah the governor, Ezra the priest and teacher of the Law, and the Levites who were instructing the people said to them all, 'This day is holy to the LORD your God. Do not mourn or weep.' For all the people had been weeping as they listened to the words of the Law.

Nehemiah said, 'Go and enjoy choice food and sweet drinks, and send some to those who have nothing prepared. This day is holy to our Lord. Do not grieve, for the joy of the LORD is your strength.'

The Levites calmed all the people, saying, 'Be still, for this is a holy day. Do not grieve.'

Then all the people went away to eat and drink, to send portions of food and to celebrate with great joy, because they now understood the words that had been made known to them.

Section A:
The Word of God
and the heart of preaching

Warm-up

I love the initiative across college campuses around the world to place Gospels in the hands of non-Christian students – a project once described to me as placing small explosives that will radically change hearts and minds. I love it when I'm visiting a guest house or hotel and discover a Gideon's Bible, and am reminded of the stories of lives turned round by opening the Bible's pages and meeting the living God. I love it when, in sad or joyful moments, hard or uncertain times, I read the Scriptures and find my life reorientated towards a different story, another reading of reality. I love it when I sit with a congregation, large or small, and together we are drawn into God's presence as the Bible is explained and we are challenged in our discipleship, provoked in our worship and encouraged in our spiritual lives. The Word of God is dynamic, changing hearts and minds, restoring broken lives, renewing churches and even whole communities.

Can you imagine the mood of the people gathered in Jerusalem's city centre that day? Having finally returned home after years of exile in a pagan land, they longed for restoration – not just the rebuilding of the broken walls of the city, but the restoration of families, the restoration of the nation itself. Nehemiah 8 introduces us to a remarkable encounter, when God's people started their journey of renewal.

The story in chapter 8, placed at the centre of Nehemiah's memoirs, signals that, with the building of the walls of Jerusalem now complete, the true foundation for the restored community would be God's Word. Nehemiah knew how strategic this would be, and so he ensures that Ezra the scholar-teacher now comes to the fore.

There are two features of the text which demonstrate that Ezra and Nehemiah saw the Word as the foundation for all that was to follow: the *centrality* and the *authority* of the Word.

The centrality of the Word

For God's people, the seventh month was one of great religious festivity, and their first act was to call for the book. It was a grassroots desire that the law should be read: 'All the people came together as one in the square before the Water Gate. They told Ezra the teacher of the Law to bring out the Book of the Law of Moses, which the LORD had commanded for Israel.' And the law commanded the attention of everyone – 'and all the people listened attentively to the Book of the Law' (verse 3); and verse 13: 'On the second day of the month, the heads of all the families, along with the priests and the Levites, gathered round Ezra the teacher of the Law to give attention to the words of the Law.'

This book retained its central place right through to the end of the month. 'They stood where they were and read from the Book of the Law of the LORD their God for a quarter of the day, and spent another quarter in confession and in worshipping the LORD their God' (Nehemiah 9:3). The Word of God represented the foundation articles, the new constitution of the people of God. It defined their identity and was placed at the very centre as they embarked on the restoration programme to which Ezra and Nehemiah were calling them. For a nation seeking its identity and shaping its programme of restoration, the Word of God mattered hugely. There is even something symbolic in the fact that it was not read in the temple, but down town: 'He read it aloud from daybreak till noon as he faced the square before the Water Gate' (verse 3).

The same is true for preaching today. Our task is not to stand in front of the Bible text, but behind it, ensuring that it is doing the talking. Too often, it seems that the Bible is peripheral rather than central, and in the preacher's attempts to be relevant, the text forms the launch pad from which the rest of the sermon takes off. So, one of the issues that we now face in churches around the world is this: *how do we restore the dynamic place of the Bible?* And the reason why this is paramount is linked to a second aspect of God's Word, which again we see in Nehemiah 8.

The authority of the Word

Here, we simply note the emphasis of verse 1: 'They told Ezra the teacher of the Law to bring out the Book of the Law of Moses, which the LORD had commanded for Israel.' The human authorship is acknowledged on several occasions: the reading was from the books of Moses. But its divine authority is emphasized: the law of God, the revelation given by him. The law was 'teaching' from God himself. Without this sense of divine authority, it would simply be the veneration of a book. There is a wonderful explanation of this in the New Testament, where Paul describes the way in which the believers received the gospel:

> And we also thank God continually because, when you received the word of God, which you heard from us, you accepted it not as a human word, but as it actually is, the word of God, which is indeed at work in you who believe.
> (1 Thessalonians 2:13)

There are several implications about the Bible to be drawn from Paul's statement:

Its authority: it is the Word 'of God'. This is very emphatic in the way in which Paul wrote it. The message of the apostles is authoritative because it originates with God himself.

Its power: 'which is indeed at work in you who believe'. It is powerful precisely because it is God's Word. We should never drive a wedge between the written Word and the living God who speaks that Word. By God's Spirit, it is powerful, life-giving and life-transforming. It goes on working in those who go on believing.

Its reception: Paul thanks God that the Thessalonian believers 'accepted it' as God's Word. He uses two words in verse 13 – they 'received' the Word, which means they heard it, but then they 'accepted' it, welcomed it in as a friend. It became part of them, continuing its work in their lives.

Its impact: Paul has already described the effect of God's Word in 1 Thessalonians 1:9, and the way in which they 'turned to God from idols to serve the living and true God'. Similarly, the impact is described in 1:8: 'The Lord's message rang out from you not only in Macedonia and Achaia – your faith in God has become known everywhere.'

This is a wonderful example of God's transforming Word, operating amongst the Thessalonians in the same way as it did amongst God's people standing in the square in Jerusalem in Nehemiah's day. The Word of God is not simply made up of propositions, distant and cold, but it is a dynamic Word that by the power of God's Spirit turns us around to serve God and shapes the way in which we are to live.

What lessons can we draw about biblical preaching today? I will highlight three principles in the next few chapters: biblical preaching must be *centred on God's Word*, must *pray God's Word* and must *understand God's Word*.

1

Biblical preaching must be centred on God's Word

The author and global preacher, John Stott, once commented that 'the secret of preaching is not so much mastering certain techniques, as being mastered by certain convictions'. And there is no more significant conviction by which to be mastered than this: the Word of God is authoritative and powerful because it is God's inspired revelation to all people, cultures and generations. As we have seen from Nehemiah's account, Scripture is *given* by God – 'which the LORD had commanded' (Nehemiah 8:1) – and must therefore set the agenda for all preaching. Our job is to ensure that we allow Scripture to be at the centre, to work hard at understanding its meaning and intent, and to devote our energies to expounding its truth.

Submitting to the Word of the Lord

1. *Authority*
In some cultures, the preacher is perceived to have authority because he has the right theological credentials. Or perhaps,

he has the right ecclesiastical title or status. Or we think his authority comes from wearing certain clothes or speaking from an elevated pulpit.

Not so. Authority comes from one primary source. When we look at the New Testament words for preaching, it is clear that they point towards one issue: preaching is not announcing our own words in our authority, but proclaiming God's Word with his authority. Many years ago, Edmund Clowney highlighted the four words which help us understand the nature of preaching.[1]

The most common word group means to declare as a herald. Preaching is to proclaim the message, which is given with the authority of the God who sends us. The message is not generated by the messenger, but by God himself. The second word is related to announcing the good news. It is not used exclusively of the task of evangelism, though it includes this. Again, it is God's good news, not ours. The third group of words relates to the task of witnessing or testifying to the facts. And the fourth word, often translated 'teaching', is to lay out the facts as God has revealed them. The significant thing to notice is not only the way in which the words are often placed alongside one another (which means that preaching will contain all of these different elements and should not be narrowly defined), but the emphasis on the 'given-ness' of the message. We are to proclaim the Word of the Lord.

Also, if we look at Paul's instructions to Timothy, we see how insistent he was that the pastoral task should involve faithful, urgent, sustained reading and proclamation of that Word (1 Timothy 4:11–16; 2 Timothy 4:1–5). 'Preach the word' or 'Proclaim the message' (2 Timothy 4:2). Here, Paul is emphasizing the heraldic declaration of what God has revealed to us in Scripture. And his additional verbs – 'correct, rebuke and encourage' – indicate that this task is purposeful: we expound God's Word in order to bring about change (as we shall see in chapters 8 – 10).

Paul's previous paragraph underlines this, with the clearest statement of why we must rely on Scripture and expound it faithfully (2 Timothy 3:14–17). The Scriptures are authoritative because they are God-breathed (verse 16), and therefore they are the only source of revelation concerning humankind's greatest need ('to make you wise for salvation'). Hence, the preaching task is to open up these Scriptures for the purpose of 'teaching, rebuking, correcting and training in righteousness' (verse 16). So, Paul presses home the point: our task is to proclaim the Bible. Nothing else will do, for nothing else reveals God's purposes, and nothing else has such transforming power. In this way, the Bible passage establishes the preacher's authority. Preaching is not authoritative because of personality, academic study or communication skills.

The great preacher Campbell Morgan made the point clearly: 'My sermon has no authority in it at all, except as an interpretation or an exposition or an illustration of the truth which is in the text. The text is everything. That is the point of authority.'

2. Integrity

Most preachers are familiar with looking at a Bible passage 'in order to grab the first preachable lesson that pops up', as David Day has written.[2] The text, in other words, offers us a pretext. It's an excuse to preach on a topic or theme dear to our hearts, which, by a stroke of luck, appears in the passage. But this is to use the Bible as a peg on which to hang our thoughts. If preachers do this, they are failing to treat it with integrity. They are not allowing the Bible to speak. But as we have seen from Nehemiah, the Word must be centre stage.

David Day urges us to 'preach on the passage, the whole passage and nothing but the passage'.[3] This is the central task for the preacher, if he truly believes in the authority of the Bible and the authority of the God who speaks it.

The apostle Paul was especially concerned that his ministry should be centred on God's Word. We know from his second letter to the Corinthians that he was being criticized by the false teachers in Corinth for a range of issues, some of which included his apparent lack of rhetorical skill. In his defence, he outlined the calling of all preachers of the Word: 'We have renounced secret and shameful ways; we do not use deception, nor do we distort the word of God. On the contrary, by setting forth the truth plainly we commend ourselves to everyone's conscience in the sight of God' (2 Corinthians 4:2).

Paul underlines his determination to be faithful to the message. He stresses a key priority: we are not to distort the Word of God, but to present its truth plainly. To 'set forth' means an open declaration, a full disclosure of the truth. It's the opposite of deception. It means 'to show your hand'. It is like the conjuror or the magician at a circus who rolls up his sleeves to show that he is hiding nothing. Paul insists we are holding nothing back, but proclaiming faithfully the whole counsel of God. And this is the force of verse 2: we don't twist the message to please our hearers, but set forth *the truth*. We don't embellish the truth to win popularity, but speak the message *plainly*. We don't reserve the message for an élite group who can be specially initiated into higher levels of spiritual experience, but commend ourselves to everyone's conscience.

Just a few verses earlier, Paul has described the characteristics of his ministry: 'Unlike so many, we do not peddle the word of God for profit. On the contrary, in Christ we speak before God with sincerity, as those sent from God' (2:17). The false teachers tried to secure converts through deception. It's possible that the preachers were similar to the occult groups of the day, salesmen who were marketing a new and mysterious religious product. Some writers think that this group objected to the way Paul spoke so openly about the gospel; they preferred truth to be shrouded in mystery. And of course, they could charge significant fees if people really would like to discover this esoteric truth. Maybe the word 'pedlar' originally referred to those who watered down wine for sale in the market. They were guilty of distorting the product, the message, but they didn't care, salesmen whose sole motive was profit.

Later, Paul gives us an insight into his concern about the defective preaching in Corinth. They used familiar language, but it was, Paul said, another Jesus, a different spirit, a different gospel (2 Corinthians 11:3–4). We are not sure what this might have represented: maybe it was a gospel that majored on strength, not weakness; a message that promised triumph, not suffering; a gospel that paraded glory, not the cross. But what really matters for Paul, and for all who are called to preach the Word, is a commitment to a faithful, clear, open declaration of the truth.

We have dwelt a while on this passage, because it so helpfully explains what we mean by Bible exposition, or expository preaching. It is simply making God's Word clear and plain, bringing out what is there. Exposition is sometimes caricatured as though it were merely a running commentary on a lengthy passage, taking four years of Sundays, for example, to preach through the whole of Leviticus. Or perhaps, we think it is a particular cultural style with three neat points held together by 'apt alliteration's artful aid'.[4] But exposition, simply defined, is opening up a Bible passage in order to expose its force and power. This is why John Stott often underlined that all true Christian preaching is expository: 'Our understanding of preaching is that it is essentially . . . an exposition of the Word of God . . . in the broad sense that it opens up the biblical text.'[5] 'In expository preaching, the biblical text is neither a conventional introduction to a sermon on a largely different theme, nor a convenient peg on which to hang a ragbag of miscellaneous thoughts, but a master which dictates and controls what is said.'[6] Let me suggest four priorities:

Four priorities

Our conviction is that Scripture is the authoritative and powerful Word of God. All preaching must be centred on God's Word if it is to prove effective in fulfilling God's purposes.

Our concern is that, if the Bible is God's Word, his voice needs to be heard. In fact, we are convinced that nothing is more important for the life of the Christian and the local church than this. Peter is bold enough to assert that those who speak should do so 'as one who speaks the very words of God' (1 Peter 4:11). Despite the human frailties of both speaker and listener, God has chosen to reveal himself and his purposes through the faithful preaching of Scripture. As I will emphasize in the next chapter, before preachers stand up to speak, they must listen carefully to his voice. In his sermons on Ephesians, John Calvin observed:

It is certain that if we come to church we shall not hear only a mortal man speaking but we shall feel . . . that God is speaking to our souls, that *he* is the teacher. He so teaches us that the human voice enters into us and so profits us that we are refreshed and nourished by it. God calls us to him as if he had his mouth open and we see him there in person.[7]

Our attitude must be to submit to God's Word, committed above all to let the Bible do the talking. In that sense, Bible exposition is not so much a method as a mindset: our attitude is one of submission to that Word, ensuring that what I am to preach flows directly from that divine revelation. And my priority, if I am a preacher, is to make that Word clear and plain.

Our approach will ensure that all preaching must take its context, content, shape and purpose from the Bible passage. We will think in subsequent chapters about how that might be achieved, but anything less than explaining clearly what the Bible says – what the Lord is saying – is not biblical preaching. The heartbeat must be the heartbeat of the Bible passage. This passage defines the message and shapes all we have to say. It is the architect's plan, quite different, mixing our metaphors, from the description Haddon Robinson once gave of preachers who merely 'salt and pepper' their messages with Bible verses.[8]

I am not referring here to a particular *style* of preaching as such. As I have implied, Bible exposition is not a specific cultural approach, with detailed verse-by-verse commentary, linear arguments and three neat points. That may work well in some contexts, but every preacher has a unique personality, cultural context and way of communicating. The core commitment is universal: we wish to expose the force and power of God's Word. At the end of your preaching (if you are a preacher), whatever your cultural style, the really important question is this: have the listeners heard the message and meaning of the Bible text itself? We have already emphasized the primary importance of preaching from a Bible passage, but it is helpful in church life sometimes to speak on a particular topic, and then we will need to range across more than one section of the Bible. But even then, there is wisdom in anchoring the sermon in one significant Bible passage, enabling hearers to focus clearly, and helping them to understand that we are not just preaching our own opinions on the topic, but finding out what God has to say about it.

3. Humility

Being convinced of the authority and centrality of the Word will also shape the preacher's own approach and motivation to the task of preaching. We have already seen from 2 Corinthians 4 that Paul was concerned to speak the Word faithfully and clearly, and to keep that central. In the same chapter, he assured the Corinthians that he was not in the business of Christian ministry to impress the crowds, to build his own power base or to feed his own ego. Paul expressed it with characteristic directness: 'What we preach is not ourselves, but Jesus Christ as Lord' (2 Corinthians 4:5).

As globalization took hold at the end of the twentieth century, some Christian commentators suggested that, at least in some parts of the Western world, a consumerist attitude was emerging in the church. This was described as a 'McChurch mentality', which was pushing Christian leaders and pastors to market themselves and their church in an almost competitive spirit. It suggested that congregations approached sermons in much the same way as they approached fast-food restaurants. Today, McDonald's; tomorrow, Burger King.

In Paul's day, there was certainly a problem with personality cults and a drive towards showmanship. Paul uses the words of his critics in 2 Corinthians 10:10: 'In person he is unimpressive and his speaking amounts to nothing.' And in the next chapter, he admits, 'I may indeed be untrained as a speaker' (11:6). His rivals in Corinth were clearly very concerned about image, projecting themselves, their eloquence and their rhetorical skill. And Paul was not afraid to confront that directly: 'What we preach is not ourselves' (4:5). We are not projecting our personalities, not trying to build our own power base. He had already said this very directly in his first letter: 'When I came to you, I did not come with eloquence or human wisdom . . . For I resolved to know nothing while I was with you except Jesus Christ and him crucified' (1 Corinthians 2:1–2).

In chapter 11, we will look more directly at the call to preach Christ. The point to underline here is that, if Scripture is at the centre, then preaching will not focus on us. Paul wanted nothing to get in the way of the gospel message. It was the authoritative proclamation that really mattered. In a media-conscious age, it is no surprise that our churches can become theatres where performance matters more than content, where we honour our evangelical 'heroes' and elevate their ministries. Christ and his Word must be centre stage.

4. *Community*
One of the significant benefits of Bible exposition is that it encourages the congregation to focus on the Bible passage, to explore and understand its significance, and to check what the preacher is saying against what they themselves are reading. Preaching, as we shall see in chapter 8, is a community event. The preacher's concern is to bring the Bible to the congregation, not simply to deliver his own conclusions, but

to encourage each person to encounter the Word of the Lord, and the Lord of that Word. Careful explanation of the Bible passage is not intended solely to provide a meal; it is also to demonstrate how to cook, so that each Christian can discover ways in which a Bible passage might be opened up. Note the commendable example of the Bereans, who 'received the message with great eagerness and examined the Scriptures every day to see if what Paul said was true' (Acts 17:11).

There is special value for the congregation if the church commits to preaching through Bible books, working consecutively across selected passages. Christopher Ash sets out a series of reasons why such preaching ministry is helpful. It ensures that the church hears the whole counsel of God and receives a rich diet; it means that preachers treat the Bible with integrity as they preach passages in their context, and thereby provide Christians with a good model for their own Bible reading.[9]

> *Careful explanation of the Bible passage is not intended solely to provide a meal; it is also to demonstrate how to cook.*

We can also ensure that the Bible is at the centre of our church life by taking seriously Paul's encouragement to Timothy: 'Devote yourself to the public reading of Scripture, to preaching and to teaching' (1 Timothy 4:13). The loss of the Word's centrality in churches is seen in many ways, including its marginalization when it is not read publicly, but also in the ever-decreasing length of time devoted to its teaching. It has been estimated that the average sermon length in UK churches has now fallen to fifteen minutes, leading one journalist to comment wryly that 'this is a remarkable tribute to the power of intercessory prayer' (that is, prayer for shorter sermons!). Congregations must play their part in ensuring that the Word is central – in its public reading as the church gathers, in appropriate and creative approaches for children's events, in family life, and in personal spiritual disciplines. The warm guidance of Deuteronomy 6 still applies: 'These commandments that I give you today are to be on your hearts. Impress them on your children. Talk about them when you sit at home and when you walk along the road, when you lie down and when you get up' (Deuteronomy 6:6–7).

Meeting the Lord of the Word

As the people gathered in Jerusalem and the Scriptures were opened (Nehemiah 8:1–2), they didn't merely listen to the words of the law, but met the God who spoke them. The dramatic encounter on the road to Emmaus, which we saw in the Introduction, makes the same point. Having met Christ through the pages of the Old Testament, the disciples declared, 'Were not our hearts burning within us while he talked with us on the road and opened the Scriptures to us?' (Luke 24:32). And breath-taking though it might seem, when God's Word is opened faithfully in our congregations, the same experience is possible today. Indeed, should that not be our prayer and expectation? Should we not long for burning hearts as we encounter the living God for ourselves?

Recent surveys amongst UK congregations indicate that the vast majority of believers come to church with high expectations, longing to hear the Word of the Lord and to meet the Lord of the Word. Yet often, we know this hope is not realized. Greg Haslam tells the story of a Native American who visited a large North American church to hear a well-known pastor preach. 'He held forth for about forty minutes to a congregation of five or six thousand people, while the

Red Indian[10] sat expressionless, his arms folded across his chest, listening very carefully. Afterwards, his host said, "Well, what did you think?" The Indian paused for a moment before saying, "Big wind. Loud thunder. No fire."' Greg Haslam uses the story in the context of his concern about the spiritual state of our churches, and the urgent need to meet God in the power of the Word and the Spirit.[11]

Preaching the Word certainly operates at the horizontal level – preacher to congregation – with the purpose of mutual edification. But we should learn from Nehemiah 8 that the purpose in opening the Word is to encounter the living God. In Jerusalem that day, the people lifted up their hands in adoration and bowed their heads in confession. All ministries of the Word, preaching included, should bring us into a deeper knowledge and experience of God through Christ. Preaching should be the occasion when God comes to us, is present with us and speaks to us. Just as on that remarkable day in Jerusalem, when we open the Bible in our churches and hear that Word proclaimed, we can truly encounter the living God.

2

Biblical preaching must pray God's Word

Charles Spurgeon, the great nineteenth-century Baptist preacher, once used an illustration that resonates with me in more ways than one. (I should explain at this point that I am slightly disabled because of polio.) He spoke of the minister who limps along like a lame man with unequal legs, for 'his praying is shorter than his preaching'. Few preachers will fail to grasp the point, for praying can often be the final step before preaching, rather than the first. And in this chapter, I would like to use the word 'pray' to imply something much deeper than a brisk request for the Lord's help and blessing. Rather, I use it to describe an attitude towards the Scriptures that implies humility before the Lord, expectancy that he should speak and a deliberate commitment to listen, think and pray as we engage wholeheartedly with the passage open in front of us.

If preaching is to place the Bible at the centre, and if our task is to open up its message, then those who preach need to be wholeheartedly committed to immersing themselves in Scripture. Michael Quicke is surely right when he suggests that the command to 'love God with all our heart, and with all our soul and with all our strength and with all our mind' also applies to our engagement with the Word of God. He writes,

> Such engagement involves not just knowing about Scripture, having a grasp of its contents, but being immersed in its life, grasped by its power, involved in its story, and convicted by its word. A preacher's relationship with Scripture is interactive and needs a vocabulary with words such as immerse, listen, question, visualize, enter, taste, experience, love, and obey.[1]

There are no short cuts. Many other things will crowd in to exclude the study, prayer and meditation which good preaching requires. I have no doubt at all that this will be a constant challenge. I know ministers are sometimes criticized for hiding away in their studies, 'six days invisible, one day incomprehensible'. But thoughtful, prayerful study is vital. The apostles soon discovered that many things distracted them from the priority of the Word and prayer (Acts 6:1–7), and that they needed to take action to ensure that first things were indeed first.

The same commitment is underlined in Paul's encouragements in the Pastoral Epistles: 'Devote yourself to the public reading of Scripture, to preaching and to teaching . . . Be diligent in these matters; give yourself wholly to them, so that everyone may see your progress. Watch your life and doctrine closely' (1 Timothy 4:13–16). Biblical preaching requires that we immerse ourselves, reading whole Bible books, reading through the passage on which we are to preach many times, diligently studying, quietly listening, prayerfully engaging with the Lord, as well as with his Word.

In this chapter, we are exploring an essential first discipline for all preachers, and for all Christians committed to hearing the Word of the Lord. It is to *pray that Word*. I first learned the value of this approach amongst believers in Latin America. My friend and colleague Igor Améstegui would frequently call together preachers in various countries as part of the work of Langham Predicación in the continent. The first act each morning would be to pray the Word. Opening the passage that we were to study that day, he would lead us together in the four steps of 'praying the Word'. They were:

- Reading in order to listen to God's voice
- Being quiet in order to meditate
- Imagining in order to identify with the text
- Praying in order to respond to God

This approach was of course founded on the fundamental conviction already underlined: that the Bible passage is the authoritative Word of God through which he still speaks. And the practice of quiet listening and meditating, identifying with the text (and the people and situations it describes) and praying in response, makes the entire exercise one that is centred on the author of the passage, God himself. It is theocentric.

Home groups and congregations

I have since used this simple approach both for personal study in preparation for preaching, but also in home groups and Bible discussions when we read the passage several times, using different translations, if available. We then allow for a period of quiet meditation and reflection. And then we reread the passage in small sections, pausing after each one to allow two or three people to pray as prompted by the themes. This is a way of reading which allows God's Word to set the agenda, to truly enter our bloodstream and to bring us into God's presence. The purpose of such reading is well expressed by Merrill Tenney. He defines the devotional study of the Bible as 'not so much a technique as a spirit; it is the spirit of eagerness which seeks the mind of God; it is the spirit of humility which listens to the voice of God; it is the spirit of adventure which pursues earnestly the will of God; it is the spirit of adoration which rests in the presence of God'.[2] It is the starting point in the process of preparing to preach, as well as a foundational discipline for all Christian disciples in listening to Scripture.

In Jesus' parable in Luke 8, the word 'hear' is used nine times in the first twenty-one verses. Of course, this means more than simply just listening to words. 'Hearing' means listening with spiritual receptivity. The value of the simple disciplines I have described above has been recognized widely across the spectrum of Christian tradition in recent years, but for the purposes of this chapter, I will summarize them more simply under three headings: *careful listening, reflective thinking and honest praying.*[3] As we approach a Bible passage, these elements belong together, and are to be performed, pen in hand, as we begin the process of immersing ourselves in Scripture, seeking to ask what it says and what it means.

Life-giving disciplines

1. *Careful listening*
We are all familiar with different types of listening. I was once speaking to someone who asked me about the health of my parents-in-law. I replied that things weren't too good, sadly, but I could tell that his mind was elsewhere. He didn't acknowledge what I had said, but went straight on to ask me for something he needed. It was disappointing, but we can all

do this: we listen to the words, but we are really formulating what *we* are going to say next. It's in one ear and out the other. But what if one morning, as you waken to the sound of a news programme on the radio, the announcer suddenly interrupts with an SOS message, and mentions your name, yes, you, as the person they are trying to reach because of a dangerously ill relative? You not only hear, but your mind – your whole person – absorbs the message and immediately responds.

God is the speaking God, and the speaking God calls for a listening people. So here's an important question: *How is your hearing?* Hebrews 3 is a text where hearing God's voice is a very urgent matter indeed. It's a very insistent piece of writing:

So, as the Holy Spirit says:

'Today, if you hear his voice,
   do not harden your hearts.'
(Hebrews 3:7–8)

And it's pressed home again a few verses later:

As has just been said:

'Today, if you hear his voice,
   do not harden your hearts.'
(Hebrews 3:15)

And just in case we missed it, it's there in the next chapter too (Hebrews 4:7). Perhaps the better question is not: 'How is your *hearing*?', but: 'How is your *heart*?', since that seems to be the core concern of the writer. The key to the passage relates to different attitudes towards hearing God's call, to responding to God's Word: 'See to it, brothers and sisters, that none of you has a sinful, unbelieving heart that turns away from the living God' (Hebrews 3:12).

In fact, the Scriptures were truly designed to be listened to, whether in synagogues or in the early Christian assemblies, and, I believe, more needs to be done to reinstate the public reading of Scripture in our churches today. But cultivating the listening and responsive heart is the very essence of good Bible reading. These days, of course, the idea of waiting and listening is completely counter-cultural. In the West, we have become addicted to speed; we demand instant everything. We live in an age of what a Microsoft researcher, Linda Stone, called 'continuous partial attention'. It means that while you are answering your email and talking to your child, your cell phone rings and you embark on another conversation. You are now involved in a continuous flow of interactions, in which you can only partially concentrate on each one. But finding the opportunity to step aside from the distracted restlessness of our world and hearts is a vital ingredient in living the life of faith. Yet, it's not easy, is it?

God is the speaking God, and the speaking God calls for a listening people.

The prophet Habakkuk was distracted too. As he looked at his society, he was dismayed by its corruption and, worse still, when he looked at God's actions in the world of his day, they made no sense at all. The story of his short book is that the most important thing for him to do was to listen to God's Word. And so, after all his questions, the struggles and the perplexity of chapter 1, Habakkuk records his determined resolve:

I will stand at my watch
   and station myself on the ramparts;
I will look to see what he will say to me,
   and what answer I am to give to this complaint.
(Habakkuk 2:1)

He needed a clear view of what was happening, a restored perspective. He wanted no distractions, and so he climbed above the city, beyond the daily reminders of violence and injustice he found there, and listened for the Word of the Lord: 'I will stand at my watch . . . I will look to see what he will say to me.' This verse hints at the same paradox as was once expressed by David Jackman in his advice to preachers: 'Learning to listen by opening our eyes is one of the key skills for the biblical preacher to develop.'[4] The verse implies an active, persevering, earnest waiting for God's Word, important qualities in our own spiritual lives and Christian community today.

Habakkuk's sense of expectancy that day in Jerusalem was the same as the one we have already seen in Jerusalem some years later, when Ezra stood at the Water Gate and read from the book of the law. And on that day (quite unlike Habakkuk's Jerusalem), the people were desperate to hear and to obey. Their eagerness and expectancy is expressed in the fact that 'all the people *listened attentively* to the book of the law' (Nehemiah 8:3, italics mine). All stood up when it was opened, longing to hear the Word of the Lord (Nehemiah 8:5). We need to ensure that this attitude of listening is an integral part of our church life, our daily discipleship and our preparation for preaching. It seems that the main reason for our sense of spiritual dryness or stagnation is that we have stopped truly listening to God, and this is what surely lies behind the poverty of preaching. Listening should always come before speaking.

One of Isaiah's songs describes how the servant of the Lord speaks about his relationship to God and his Word:

> The Sovereign LORD has given me a well-instructed tongue,
>   to know the word that sustains the weary.
> He wakens me morning by morning,
>   wakens my ear to listen like one being instructed.
> The Sovereign LORD has opened my ears;
>   I have not been rebellious,
>   I have not turned away.
> (Isaiah 50:4–5)

The servant learns to listen before he speaks. Here is a daily discipline of listening to God before speaking on behalf of him, an attitude basic in all preaching – and for all true disciples.

But it seems to be a rare quality. Too often we are driven by an activist mentality that has little time for listening, or we come to the Bible for quick solutions and easy answers. Preachers often experience panic on Saturday night, urgently scouring the passage for something to say the following morning. But listening can be nurtured; we get better by working at it.

One important practical step is to learn to read slowly. The story is told of Sidney Piddington, who was confined for three years in a Japanese prisoner-of-war camp in Singapore, with very limited access to reading material. Whilst there, he discovered what he called 'the special joy of super-slow reading', lingering over each page and entering into the experience being described by the author. As Eugene Peterson reminds us, Jesus' first parable in each of the three Synoptic Gospels emphasizes that the centrality of the Word of God in our lives 'is not about reading but about listening: "Let anyone with ears to hear listen!" (cf. Matt 13:3–9; Mark 4:3–9; Luke 8:5–8)'.

Peterson continues: 'The punch line of each of John of Patmos's sermons to his seven churches is similar: "Let anyone who has an ear listen to what the Spirit is saying to the churches" (Revelation 2:7, 11, 17, 29; 3:6, 13, 22 NRSV).'[5]

2. Reflective thinking

There is a second discipline that we need to exercise, once again with the Bible passage open and with a sustained commitment to listening in God's presence. This is traditionally referred to as 'meditation', but the word suffers from some unhelpful stereotyping which can lead to dangerous mistakes. Some imagine that meditation means we need to empty ourselves, but Christian meditation is in fact the opposite. It is not emptying our minds, but bringing our whole selves to focus on God as revealed in his Word. And again, it is not inappropriate to have a notebook and pen to hand, as we seek to understand the meaning and message of the text, and, if we are preachers, to gather first ideas which will help shape the preaching of that passage.

One of the most instructive sections of Scripture on this theme is Psalm 119. It demonstrates the importance of reflective thinking, both in its structure and its content:

> Oh, how I love your law!
>   I meditate on it all day long . . .
> How sweet are your words to my taste,
>   sweeter than honey to my mouth!
> (Psalm 119:97, 103)

There is a sequence here that is worth noting. In verse 97, the psalmist describes his delight in the law as part of God's Word ('law' being just one of the eight different words the poet uses for God's Word). But as Chris Wright has pointed out in his expositions of Psalm 119, for the heart to love God's Word, the mind has to think about it, and the memory has to store it. Psalm 119 was not designed for speed-reading. So, 'I meditate on it all day long'; 'Your commands are always with me.' The verses imply that the Lord's teaching has truly become a part of him. He expresses this earlier in the psalm:

> I have hidden your word in my heart
>> that I might not sin against you . . .
> I meditate on your precepts
>> and consider your ways.
> I delight in your decrees;
>> I will not neglect your word.
> (Psalm 119:11, 15–16).

In the Old Testament, the heart is the seat of thinking. Thinking is hard work, and in the New Testament, Paul urges that Timothy be diligent, correctly handling the Word (2 Timothy 2:15). And it is the same in this psalm. Reading the Bible requires reflective thinking and calls for a chewing over of the text. It might often be rigorous and sustained thought, as we ponder the meaning of a passage through the day, maybe in the midst of other duties. This is where the psalmist's emphasis on 'storing up' Scripture is part of the discipline.

As a child, I was encouraged to memorize sections of the Bible, a discipline for which I am very grateful, but which today is largely lost (in English-speaking cultures perhaps because of the multiplicity of Bible translations). As a student, I would carry in my jacket pocket a series of small index cards on which I had scribbled Bible passages. They were nuggets of truth that became embedded in my heart and mind. I wish I had committed much more to memory. Such reflective thinking can be described with words such as 'tasting', 'savouring', 'chewing', 'ruminating'. Often, it takes some effort before the text yields some nourishment. John Stott spoke of the task of reading a Bible passage in this way: 'Probe your text, like a bee with a spring blossom, or like a humming-bird probing a hibiscus flower for its nectar. Worry at it like a dog with a bone. Suck it as a child sucks an orange. Chew it as a cow chews the cud.'[6]

I wonder to what extent we follow the psalmist's example. The danger is that we adopt the mentality of so much of our Westernizing global culture which specializes in the sound bite and lives off fast food. In our world, many things are being downsized and miniaturized. A church leader in Canterbury has slimmed down the Bible to fifty-seven pages, which, as one reviewer has said, 'those in a hurry to be born again can cram into their heads in 100 minutes'. Then there is the SMS Bible devised in Australia: 31,713 verses translated into short text messages to pass on to your friends. But, as we know, all Christians – preachers most of all – must engage with God's Word, developing the basic disciplines of listening, thinking, chewing, memorizing, meditating. By implication, this means that our reading is sustained, and that God's Word is held in our hearts and minds (Deuteronomy 6:6–9; Proverbs 3:21–24; 6:22).

Through such reflective thinking, we are entering into the text, and the text is entering into us. We are truly taking it to heart, digesting and absorbing it, just as Jeremiah, Ezekiel and John graphically expressed the way in which they assimilated God's Word such that it truly became a part of them: 'When your words came, I ate them; they were my joy and my heart's delight' (Jeremiah 15:16); 'He said to me, "Son of man, eat this scroll I am giving you and fill your stomach with it." So I ate it, and it tasted as sweet as honey in my mouth' (Ezekiel 3:3); 'So I went to the angel and asked him to give me the little scroll. He said to me, "Take it and eat it. It will turn your stomach sour, but 'in your mouth it will be as sweet as honey'" ' (Revelation 10:9).

3. Honest praying

The third element is one of response. We should not see each of these disciplines as a linear progression, because often they will overlap in a multi-layered way. Our response to the Word is likely to be continuous, not simply 'stage 3'. Part of reading involves honest praying: we engage in what we are hearing by *praying the passage*. That makes sense, because reading the Bible is relational and therefore conversational. It demands our participation with the author himself. Jim Packer once asked, 'How can we turn our knowledge *about* God into knowledge *of* God? The rule for doing this is demanding but simple. It is that we turn each truth that we learn *about* God into a matter of meditation *before God*, leading to prayer and praise *to* God.'[7]

It's not unusual to hear Christians say that, before their conversion to Christ, the Bible was a closed book. On coming to faith, they began to discover its riches, and this was because it is a matter of relationship. If you stand outside a church building, looking at its stained-glass window, you see nothing of its rich colour and design. You can see the colour and beauty only when you are viewing the window from the inside. Or, if you are reading a map, you are most likely to understand it – to recognize the landforms – once you are travelling on the road. In the same way, truly entering the Bible text requires that we are on the inside, that we are travelling the road, that we know the author. It was this basic issue that led Tyndale rightly to suggest that even a ploughboy with the Bible could know more of God than the most learned religious academic who ignored its author. It is all a matter of relationship, and reading its pages should be the doorway into God's presence and therefore the best stimulus to conversation with him. Again, Psalm 119 helps us, since the whole of this Psalm is a prayer. Its basic thrust is an appeal for understanding:

> I have more insight than all my teachers,
>> for I meditate on your statutes.
> I have more understanding than the elders,
>> for I obey your precepts.
> (Psalm 119:99–100)

The psalmist's favourite prayer is for understanding. He longs for the Lord's teaching, recognizing that God's Word is the wisdom that counts, and that without such illumination, he is lost. If God is the fountain of all wisdom, and if God reveals his wisdom in his Word and through his Son, then this kind of prayer-reading is a priority. It is God who teaches us, God who opens our eyes (Psalm 119:102). Paul says the same: 'Where is the wise person? Where is the teacher of the law? Where is the philosopher of this age? . . . We declare God's wisdom . . . things God has revealed to us by his Spirit' (1 Corinthians 1:20; 2:7, 10). It is God's work of illumination (Ephesians 3:16–19).

With the Word in our hearts and minds, and the Spirit alongside us, responsive prayer will have a variety of elements. It will at times be an honest expression of our struggle to understand, or to enter God's presence; it will at other times be an urgent request for his help; it will often be a response of adoration or worship. For we are engaging not simply with the text, but with the Lord who has spoken that Word. That is the kind of Bible reading that really matters, for it calls us into relationship with the living God. Time devoted to such reading of a Bible passage is essential if we are truly to understand its meaning and message. We will not yet have opened Bible commentaries nor studied every detail, but we have humbly and diligently opened heart and mind, to seek not just the message, but the author himself.

This is the task of the whole church, not just the preacher. A prayerful, expectant reading of God's Word is central to Christian worship, as we will explore later. And praying the Word is a necessary foundation to preparing to preach.

John Stott once gave a clue to his preparation, which perhaps partly explains the effectiveness of his preaching.

> I have always found it helpful to do as much of my sermon preparation as possible on my knees, with the Bible open before me, in prayerful study. This is not because I am a bibliolater and worship the Bible; but because I worship the God of the Bible and desire to humble myself before him and his revelation. Even while I am giving my mind to the study of the text, I pray earnestly that the eyes of my heart may be enlightened.[8]

3

Biblical preaching must understand
God's Word

'Exegesis is loving God enough to stop and listen carefully to what he says,' claims Eugene Peterson.[1]

That's a great perspective on how to study Scripture. Exegesis is seeking to understand the words, ideas and meaning of a passage, and Peterson's point is that such study is not the dull pursuit of technical jargon, but the way to encounter God and hear his voice. Seen in this light, the work of understanding God's Word is a demanding but a truly joyful and fulfilling task.

A Christian software company recently advertised a CD full of useful material for studying the Bible. Welcome though such material can be, the selling line in the advertisement was disappointing: 'Less time studying, more time living.' A shade manipulative perhaps, and certainly misleading, since it suggests that study time should be minimized.

To recap: the Word of God must be central to our lives, our churches and our preaching (chapter 1); it's important to pray that Word, immersing ourselves in Scripture in order to hear the Lord's voice (chapter 2). Now, let's look at the task of understanding the message of God's Word.

Ezra is central to the story in Nehemiah 8. Here was a remarkable teacher who combined three key disciplines: 'For Ezra had devoted himself to the study and observance of the Law of the LORD, and to teaching its decrees and laws in Israel' (Ezra 7:10). The verse encapsulates a wonderful trilogy: Ezra was committed to study, observe and teach. In chapter 7, we will explore the commitment to observe or obey the Word. But Ezra could not have taught this Word to the congregation in Jerusalem unless he had first devoted himself to its careful study. The same emphasis is seen in Paul's encouragement to Timothy. His instructions to the young leader, confronting a variety of challenges in the Ephesian church, include the call to be serious in the way he handles the Scriptures: 'Command and teach these things . . . devote yourself to the public reading of Scripture, to preaching and to teaching. Do not neglect your gift . . . Be diligent in these matters; give yourself wholly to them, so that everyone may see your progress . . . Persevere in them . . .' (1 Timothy 4:11–16). Timothy's understanding of 'these things', a phrase that occurs eight times in the letter, sums up the instructions Paul gave Timothy, which he was to pass to the church in Ephesus. That is, Timothy was to pass on Paul's teaching, so it was vitally important that Timothy understood 'these things'. His responsible leadership of the church demanded focused diligence in his reading and study of the Scriptures and his careful teaching of apostolic truth.

Such diligent study of the Bible certainly does not contradict the emphasis on prayerful reflection which we highlighted in the last chapter. The two ways always belong together. Our understanding of God's Word is dependent on the illumination of his Spirit. It was for this reason that Paul encouraged Timothy to 'reflect on what I am saying' – which would demand careful thought – 'for the Lord will give you insight into all this' – which would demand prayerful dependence (2 Timothy 2:7).

The emphasis in many churches on providing 'Bible overviews' for congregations has to be very welcome in an age when there is so much biblical illiteracy. Initially, we will want to take the macroscopic view, reading the whole of Scripture in order to understand its big story. As we shall see, it is essential for those who are preachers to understand the specific Bible passage from which they are to preach within the framework of the whole of Scripture, and so a fundamental discipline will be to commit ourselves to the panoramic reading of the Bible, taking in its full sweep. Many of us will already have greatly benefitted from the daily Bible reading plan first constructed by Robert Murray McCheyne, allowing us to read the whole Bible in a year (or over a longer period if that is more suitable).[2]

I once visited North India, joining a gathering of some 1,000 church planters. They met for one week each month, devoting their time to the study of a Bible book. Month by month, they studied different sections of Scripture – the book of Acts was the focus while I was with them. And given this incredible investment of one week each month, taken out of their regular work of church planting, with all of its attendant costs of travel and time, I asked the leaders why they encouraged such a commitment. They replied that the majority of church planters had been converted from a Hindu background, and so they had a Hindu worldview. Now that they were Christian believers and were founding Christian communities, it was essential that they had a biblical worldview and that they taught their newly founded congregations the truth of Scripture from Genesis to Revelation. It struck me then that such an approach was needed in my own

Western culture just as much as in the villages of Uttar Pradesh. It is needed worldwide. And it is needed for every Bible preacher today.

Growing in understanding

Understanding Scripture is foundational to the Christian life, and it is a joyful journey of discovery that will take our entire lives. We can touch on this only briefly, but we will begin with our basic understanding of the nature of the Bible itself, before then turning to the more detailed task of how to understand a specific Bible passage. And we will finish the chapter by reminding ourselves of the value of understanding God's Word in community, and not in isolation.

1. Understanding the Bible

The unique feature of the Bible is its dual authorship. It is God's authoritative and powerful Word but, through the overruling of that one author, God himself, multiple human authors in a variety of cultures and contexts have shaped the book we now hold in our hands. This immediately presents a challenge for today's readers, since the wide variety of human authors belonged to an equally wide variety of cultures and contexts, all of which seem 'foreign' to us.

Some time ago, I enjoyed reading J. B. Priestley's description of his visit to a Nonconformist chapel in Birmingham, many years after his childhood church experience. He clearly suffered from a degree of culture shock: 'I saw how odd it was that these mild Midland folk . . . should come every Sunday morning through the quiet grey streets and assemble here to wallow in wild oriental imagery.' It seemed he had stepped into another world. His description of the service captures the bewilderment of many people who read the Bible:

They sat with bent heads listening to accounts of ancient and terribly savage tribal warfare, of the lust and pride of hook-nosed and raven-bearded chieftains, of sacrifice and butchery on the glaring deserts of the Near East. They chanted in unison their hope of an immortality to be spent in cities built of blazing jewels, with fountains of milk and cascades of honey, where kings played harps while maidens clashed cymbals; and one could not help wondering what these people would do if they really did find themselves billeted for ever in this world of the Eastern religious poets. What, in short, had these sober Northern islanders to do with all this Oriental stuff? What did it, what could it really mean to them?[3]

And it's a very important question. If we are to make sense of the Bible's pages, then we are wise to remember several significant facts about its nature.

a. The Bible is a library

The Bible is made up of different types of literature – we use the word 'genre'. So, as we begin the work of understanding the Bible passage, we first need to ask what kind of writing it is. We naturally do this in everyday life. For example, when we see an advertisement for toothpaste, we know that it has a particular purpose. It is trying to persuade us to buy it, and so we should 'read' it carefully, aware of its sometimes manipulative purpose. On the other hand, when I am travelling and I receive an email from my wife, I know it is telling the truth. A leaflet from a politician is something different again. And it is the same for a poem or a novel or a railway timetable. These are very different types of literature, and we instinctively read them in the light of their genre.

The same thing needs to be learned as we come to the different parts of the biblical library. There is *narrative*, with its storyline of events and characters. Much of Scripture takes this form. There is *poetry*, with its distinct styles of construction and its compelling imagery. There is *prophecy*, to be read carefully in the light of its immediate context as well as its subsequent fulfilment. There is *wisdom*, a style of writing that reflects on the difficult questions and the practical concerns of everyday life. There are *Gospels*, a narrative form of writing, but with a clear focus on the person of Christ and containing specific theological themes. Then there are *epistles*, written to help young churches confront the challenges of growth and the opportunities of mission. And finally, *apocalyptic*, such as parts of the books of Daniel and Revelation, with their symbols and pictures, but an intention to address profound issues relating to God's ultimate purposes.

In each case, we must realize that we are listening in to a conversation taking place between the Bible author and his original listeners, and so we need to identify and rightly interpret the types of speech used. This is a substantial theme, and detailed comment is not within my present purpose, but there are many good books which explain the different types of biblical literature, and how these impact on the way in which we understand their meaning and preach their message.

b. The Bible is history

Of course, the Bible is history – a story of God's dealings with humankind, and within it many other stories. Originally, they were 'ordinary' pieces of human communication. Part of the challenge and joy of understanding these passages is that often we are hearing only one side of the conversation. It is like listening to someone engaged in an animated telephone conversation: you can only make sense of the exchange as you try to piece together what each person might be saying. And in Bible reading, this means building up a picture of the context of the author and the original 'listeners'. A key principle in understanding and preaching the Bible is that it can only properly be ours once we have allowed it fully to be theirs. So we must put ourselves in their sandals and think ourselves into their situation.

I have a friend whose father is committed to a strict exercise regime, jogging each day in order to keep fit. He recently told his son that it was healthy to do this, so why not adopt the same practice too? My friend replied that this was not biblical, paraphrasing Proverbs 28:1: 'Only the guilty run when no-one is chasing them.'

We may laugh, but this proves an important point: you can make the Bible say anything you want! So, the discipline of understanding the original context has to be an essential first step in understanding the meaning and message of a Bible passage. As we have often taught in Langham Preaching programmes around the world, we don't ask: 'What does this text mean for me now?' until we have understood as well as we possibly can: 'What did this text mean for them then?' We will turn to this in more detail shortly.

> *We must put ourselves in their sandals and think ourselves into their situation.*

c. The Bible is a unity

The fact that the Bible is the work of the one divine author means that it is a unity. Despite the great variety in human authorship, we read Scripture expecting harmony and consistency, expecting the Bible story to hang together. Again, this is a rich theme to be explored, but it is worth remembering some simple implications. In particular, we will see in chapter 11 that there is a central focus on Christ, the unifying person in all Christian interpretation of the Bible. We will learn to interpret one Bible passage in the light of another on a similar theme, especially when difficult texts need wider illumination or explanation. And we need to understand how each part of the Bible is related to the wider biblical story, the big narrative of God's purposes which Scripture articulates, from creation, to the fall, to redemption and new creation.

2. Understanding a Bible passage

A helpful way to work on a Bible passage is to use a simple grid, as below, which introduces three important areas for study: understanding a passage in context, understanding a passage in detail and understanding a passage in relation to the rest of the Bible. I first put this together after reading the helpful work of Alan Stibbs,[4] and I often use this as a simple worksheet as I begin to look at a Bible passage. (It is also reproduced as Appendix 2.)

A. Understanding a passage in context		
Literature	Author, situation, people	Author's purpose
B. Understanding a passage in detail		
Words, people, repetition, links	Divisions	Main theme
C. Understanding a passage in relation to the whole Bible		

As the grid shows, there are three main areas to explore, and we will illustrate this process by looking at a short Old Testament passage. I've chosen the closing words of Habakkuk's prophecy:

> I heard and my heart pounded,
>> my lips quivered at the sound;
> decay crept into my bones,
>> and my legs trembled.
> Yet I will wait patiently for the day of calamity
>> to come on the nation invading us.
> Though the fig-tree does not bud
>> and there are no grapes on the vines,
> though the olive crop fails
>> and the fields produce no food,
> though there are no sheep in the sheepfold
>> and no cattle in the stalls,
> yet I will rejoice in the LORD,
>> I will be joyful in God my Saviour.
> The Sovereign LORD is my strength;
>> he makes my feet like the feet of a deer,
>> he enables me to tread on the heights.

> For the director of music. On my stringed instruments.
> (Habakkuk 3:16–19)

A. Understanding the passage in context

Our first step in reading a Bible passage is to understand its original context. What type of literature is this? Who was the author; what was his situation; and to whom was he writing? And, most particularly, why was he writing? So, our purpose is to travel back to Jerusalem at the time of Nehemiah, or back to Corinth in the first century, so that we first understand the passage in that context and culture, before we can bring the message to our contemporary context.

Our sample passage from Habakkuk 3 is a well-known section from a little-known prophecy. If a preacher ventures into this short book, it is usually only to quote this remarkable doxology with which Habakkuk closes his prophecy. It is undoubtedly one of the most beautiful sections of the Old Testament, but often it is preached with relatively little regard for its context. So, here are the questions:

What kind of literature is this? We might first reply that it is prophecy, since the whole book represents the oracle or burden which Habakkuk received from the Lord (Habakkuk 1:1). But we also sense the poetic style of this short passage and, when we also note the closing phrase of verse 19 – 'on my stringed instruments' – we realize it is a song. It is an expression of worship, but sung in a remarkable situation.

And what about the author and his situation? To preach from this passage, it is essential to read the book as a whole. We soon discover from its opening chapter that Habakkuk is bewildered by the moral and spiritual collapse that he is witnessing amongst his own people in Jerusalem. Worse, when he appeals to God to intervene, it seems more terrible still: the Lord sends the ruthless Babylonians to destroy the city and carry off his own people. The short prophecy charts Habakkuk's journey, from the anxious questions of why God is allowing such terrible spiritual decline (Habakkuk 1), to the quiet waiting for his word of revelation (Habakkuk 2:1–5), to the repeated woes of judgment on the invaders and on all nations – his own included – who turn from the ways of the Lord (2:6–20), and on to the extraordinary perspective of God's actions in salvation history (3:1–15). So, the final four verses of the prophecy, frequently sung or quoted in quiet worship services, actually arise from an extraordinarily devastating series of events which shook the nation, and Habakkuk too.

So what might we conclude with regard to God's purpose? The book finds its place in Scripture because of its ultimate affirmation that the Sovereign Lord is in control of the events of history and the lives of his people. But before we can preach from this doxology, we need to drill down into the passage itself. Here is the summary of the first stage: understanding the passage in its context.

Understanding a passage in context		
Literature	Author, situation, people	Author's purpose
Prophecy Poetry A song	Habakkuk Jerusalem at the end of 7th century BC At the time of the Babylonian invasion	To discover God's sovereign purposes in the world, even in the midst of the collapse of his people

B. Understanding the passage in detail
We now work through a series of basic questions to discover the detail: are there significant words or ideas that will help us understand? Are there images and metaphors? Are there links between ideas; is there repetition of themes or words, or particular characters or illustrations? And so on . . . It is often recommended that we should read a Bible passage using our senses, so that we get a deeper understanding, living

in the story, using our imagination, but allowing it to be disciplined by the text. David Day illustrates from the dramatic story in Isaiah 6:1–13, as Isaiah enters the temple and encounters the holy God: 'What am I hearing here? Or seeing? Or smelling, touching, tasting?' It feels like an earthquake; it smells like burning flesh.[5] In this way, we can more effectively experience the mood of the passage. We should also use our senses to read Habakkuk 3:16–19 too, given its range of mood and experience.

We want to understand the writing style, and the nature of the sentences, whether commands or questions or exclamations. Then, we will need to examine the units of thought or the paragraphs, the natural blocks of text in which a single point is made or developed. Many preachers find it helpful to keep interrogating the passage – what is being said and why? – and writing summaries of content and purpose for each paragraph. It is especially helpful to examine the flow of thought from one sentence to another, since this gradually helps us understand its possible structure or storyline or argument.

In the case of Habakkuk 3:16–19, there are several things I would scribble on my sheet:

Are there some significant words?

Verse 16. 'trembled' – why does he express this 'mood' in verse 16? Perhaps because of the vision of God in the previous verses? But we also read in verse 16 a comment about 'the nation invading us', and we know from chapter 1 that this is the description of the invading Babylonian army whom God is sending in judgment on his people. No wonder he was shaking!

Verse 16. 'Yet' – a significant word that helps us interpret Habakkuk's response to what he is witnessing. It reminds me of Paul in 2 Corinthians 4:8, when he says he is 'hard pressed . . . *but* not crushed; perplexed, *but* not in despair'.

Verse 18. 'rejoice' – a repeated idea in verse 18. And after the devastation described in verse 17 (related to the judgment we read about earlier in the prophecy), the point is clear: there is nothing to rejoice in, except 'the Lord', 'the Saviour'.

Verse 19. 'the heights' – why is this significant? It seems to refer to God's strengthening him for what lies ahead. But it might also refer to the high places where pagan shrines were often built – so, God will help us overcome every spiritual challenge too.

What about the flow of thought or divisions?
Of course, this is a very short passage and we should not press divisions where they don't arise from the text. But there does seem to be a definite shift of mood – from the trembling and the quiet waiting of verse 16, to the rejoicing of verse 18, through to the more confident mood of verse 19.

Can we identify the main theme?
The passage describes several different moods, but it seems they all focus around Habakkuk's trust in the Lord – for whom he will wait (verse 16), in whom he will rejoice (verse 18), and by whom he will be strengthened (verse 19). It is centred on the Lord, the One who is in control whatever happens. Here's the summary of the second stage of our work:

Understanding a passage in detail		
Words, people, repetition, links	Divisions	Main theme
Trembled (verse 16) Yet (verse 16) Rejoice (verse 18) The heights (verse 19)	Trembling and waiting (verse 16) Rejoicing (verse 18) Confidence (verse 19)	Trusting God whatever the situation? God is in control? God is enough?

C. Understanding the passage in relation to the whole Bible

We now come to a third stage, which will help us see this passage within the wider frame of what God has said. We think of other parts of the Bible that might shed light on this one. This is important, for example, when the New Testament passage makes reference to the Old Testament; or where a story in Acts might illuminate an issue in one of Paul's epistles; or, as we hinted earlier, where one difficult passage needs to be understood within the wider context of the Bible's teaching on that theme elsewhere in Scripture.

There are various links which might need to be explored. For example, this will include how one passage is quoted in another part of the Bible, such as Habakkuk's famous statement that 'the righteous person will live by his faithfulness' (Habakkuk 2:4), which is picked up three times in the New Testament (Romans 1:17; Galatians 3:11; Hebrews 10:36–38). Following up these references will be essential in order to preach from Habakkuk 2 appropriately. Or we might need to check how common theological words or themes are used across Scripture (kingdom, judgment, redemption, salvation, God's people . . .). And then, we might also need to be aware of how the passage we are studying fits within the overall story of God's saving work throughout the Bible.

For the Habakkuk passage, there might be several sections of Scripture we would want to look at, though not necessarily refer to, in our message: we would need to read chapter 1 (at least) of Habakkuk's prophecy if we are really to understand the emotions of the concluding doxology, and why he refers to 'the nation invading us'. We might want to feel the similar emotions of Jeremiah (Jeremiah 20:7–18), who also asked God some difficult questions; or try to identify with the experience of Job, who was also bewildered by God's actions; or make reference to Paul in 2 Corinthians 4 and 12, who, like Habakkuk, discovered God's strength in the midst of weakness; or affirm Paul's confident declaration that, whatever happens, nothing can separate us from God's love and his good purposes (Romans 8:28–39). All such passages are valuable background, but need not necessarily be used in our preaching of the Habakkuk passage unless they truly serve the purpose of the sermon. Again, here's the summary:

Understanding a passage in relation to the whole Bible
Habakkuk 1; Jeremiah 20:7–18; Job; 2 Corinthians 4:7–12; 12:7–10; Romans 8:28–39

In the next two chapters, we will turn to the question of how to frame the main theme of a message and how we can preach this with clarity. For now, we summarize the process of understanding a passage, using three basic principles which were outlined by John Stott some years ago, and which explain the basics of Bible interpretation.[6]

First, *we must look at the natural meaning of a passage* (which Stott referred to as the principle of *simplicity*). We should understand it in its normal or natural sense – some writers suggest the literal sense, but that can be misleading, since Scripture often speaks figuratively, using symbols or poetic images. Did Habakkuk's bones really decay and did his feet become hinds' feet? No, these descriptions are part of the poetic force of the passage, and are obviously not literally true. So, we read the passage following the normal rules of language, allowing it to speak for itself.

Secondly, *we must look for the original meaning of the passage* (the principle of *history*). We have already given thought to what this passage referred to when Habakkuk originally wrote it down. What was the context of the 'invasion' to which he referred? Why were the fields and vineyards destroyed? We are able to understand how remarkable it was that he could 'rejoice in the LORD' once we realize the terrible context in which he sang his song.

Thirdly, *we must look for the general meaning of the passage* (the principle of *harmony*). That is, we must understand this passage in the light of the rest of the Bible, as we have already affirmed. And we can see from Jeremiah or Job or Paul – or even Jesus himself (who for the joy set before him endured the cross) – that Habakkuk's experience is one which fits the experience of the true believer.

We have still more work to do in focusing on the theme of the message we are to preach (chapter 4) and on clarifying how we should present this (chapter 5). But we should never move to those steps without first praying the Word and then doing all we can to understand it in the ways we have outlined.

3. Understanding a passage together

We conclude this chapter by once again highlighting how the congregation can engage in this same task of understanding Bible passages. I have sometimes used the simple grid we have worked on with home groups or Bible discussion groups with young people. It provides a simple but helpful guide to understanding the key elements. But I also offer one other tool that has often proved to be a great group exercise in church settings. It is sometimes referred to as 'manuscript study', and its intention is to encourage a group of Christians to work together in uncovering what a passage is saying.

What is a manuscript study of the biblical text? The manuscript format is a tool that aids the study of Scripture and so helps in the process of uncovering its meaning. A Bible passage is selected and printed out on a sheet, omitting all notes and divisions of chapter and verse. This forces us to work directly with the text alone, free from the 'sectioning' that can often govern the way we read it (paragraph, chapter, verse). We discover for ourselves how the text is structured, or what the flow of thought might be. We observe the text, paying close attention to the words that make up each sentence, and then how these sentences relate to each other as they cluster to unfold an event or idea.

The Bible passage is one block of text, with line numbers provided but no verse or paragraph divisions. We have it in front of us and can start to work on it by indicating the transition to a new paragraph, writing on the manuscript with some appropriate sign. The group is provided with coloured pens or pencils, so that they can mark it all up with underlinings, circles, connecting lines, numbers – or any device really which helps to explore the content. We can write comments and questions in the margin or between the lines. We can use coloured markers for added visual emphasis as we highlight repeated words, phrases and themes. Again, the purpose is to observe and actively work on the text, to accent what seems to be significant and to become more involved with it in a graphic way.

It is possible to keep several pages face up on a table so that the investigation of the text can always be done in visual contact with its context. This aids in the discovery of thematic developments, and often the relationship of one part to a larger unit becomes evident as the study progresses. The observation of such integrative patterns means we might be getting close to the author's intended meaning.

Of course, it is better if this is done in a group. Everyone round the table has the same text, and each person initially studies on their own. The most valuable person is the one who, coming to it for the first time, has a string of questions about the text. Questions are then asked which are authentic, not the ones to which we already have the answers. This is a very good opportunity to learn from one another. A range of observations, tested against the text, allows the meaning best supported by the text to become clear. The authority of the text is primary, as all other ideas are submitted to it. And since we are sitting together around the Bible, the impact of hearing the Word – whilst very personal – is not allowed to be merely private. The process becomes corporate.

I use this method occasionally as I come to a Bible passage on which I must preach. But why not use this method in your home group or youth group? In Appendix 3 there is a sample sheet: 'How to work on a manuscript', which gives simple instructions and is worth printing out for everyone in the group.

In this first section of the book, our first responsibility as preachers has begun – we have committed ourselves to place the Bible at the centre, to pray that Word and to understand its message. Without this foundation, preaching is empty rhetoric. But with these commitments, we are ready to move ahead to the task of opening that Word in such a way as to enable God's people to encounter the living God.

Section B:
The teacher
and the work of preaching

Warm-up

Is there a difference between reading a Bible commentary and listening to a Bible sermon?

We have much to gain from studying books about a Bible passage, and commentaries are essential tools for anyone who is committed to explain the Bible faithfully and relevantly. But listening to a preacher expound a passage should be a different experience. I speak about the ideal, of course, but preaching is not only a dynamic event – it should be a divine event. It is the occasion when God's Word, God's Spirit and God's people come together in his presence to meet with him. We will see shortly that God's people play an essential part in that dynamic, but in this section we will look at the task of the preacher in opening up the Bible to his audience. Returning to Nehemiah 8, we can see at least three

> *Preaching is not only a dynamic event – it should be a divine event.*

aspects of the work of the teacher in making sure that the Word of God came to the people of God.

Making the Word accessible

Nehemiah's memoir is extremely clear at this point. If God's Word was to be the foundation for their families, their day-to-day living, their relationships and their society, then it had to be accessible to all. We see it in the opening verses of the chapter: 'All the people came together as one' (verse 1); Ezra read before the assembly, which was made up of 'men and women and all who were able to understand' (verse 2, and repeated in verse 3); 'Ezra opened the book. All the people could see him' (verse 5); 'For all the people had been weeping as they listened to the words of the Law' (verse 9); 'On the second day of the month, the heads of all the families, along with the priests and the Levites, gathered round Ezra the teacher of the Law to give attention to the words of the Law' (verse 13).

It is clear from the repetition that Ezra wanted to make sure that everyone – men and women, young and old – had access to God's Word. It is also worth noting that verse 4 demonstrates that Ezra chose a group of others to help him with the reading of the law, something that was not just for priests or Levites. And when coupled with the location (city centre rather than temple), the fact that Ezra had a team of lay helpers only strengthens the sense, as Hugh Williamson comments, that Ezra wanted to avoid any impression that the law was the private preserve of the religious professional.[1]

Making the Word clear

The record emphasizes the effort Ezra and his team invested into making sure that everybody grasped what they were listening to. This is obvious from the start: the assembly included 'all who were able to understand' (verse 2), probably meaning children older than infancy. And Ezra's team worked hard at making the content of the law clear, 'giving the meaning so that the people understood what was being read' (verse 8). And this produced a remarkable response: 'Then all the people went away to eat and drink, to send portions of food and to celebrate with great joy, because they now understood the words that had been made known to them' (verse 12). Understanding led to celebration.

Ezra's teams worked hard to translate, interpret and explain what was being read, evidence of a sustained emphasis on making the Word accessible and clear. Ezra and Nehemiah knew how important this would be for the well-being of the community as the people settled back into Jerusalem. Nothing was more important than that men and women, young and old, tribe after tribe, heard and understood.

Involving others

One other small feature of the text is worth noting: Ezra chose a group to help him with the reading (verse 4). Verses 7 and 8 describe the teams who helped with the translation, interpretation and explanation. Why is this significant? In some cultures, the preacher or the pastor can sometimes come across as the professional, the expert. Only the pastor seems to have any right or authority to preach or teach. But one important responsibility of Bible teachers is also to help others to understand how to enjoy Scripture, through the way they handle it and involve them in it. So, we need to find ways to engage others in this task, and offer appropriate levels of training to do it well. Such team ministry is enormously valuable.

In my work with Langham Preaching, it has been exciting to see the emergence of a global network of preachers' clubs, or fellowship groups (*escuelitas* in Latin America – small preachers' schools), all designed to encourage the team to work together. Many preachers and pastors are lonely people, working at the Bible passage in isolation, and so we need to find ways to link up with others, benefit from their insights, pray together for our work, and share the task of proclaiming God's Word. (Appendix 6 includes an introduction to the purpose and content of such group meetings.)

We will turn now to some further principles that should shape the work of the preacher: biblical preaching must be *focused*, must be *clear*, must *be relevant* and must be *embodied*.

4

Biblical preaching must be focused

I often travel with an old friend. It's a Nikon 70-300mm lens. Once this is safely embedded in the camera body, I can use the through-the-lens viewfinder to focus very precisely on a distant landscape, or capture a stalking heron alongside the river Cherwell, or take a candid shot of the amusing facial contortions of a family member. There is very little need for subsequent computer editing of the photo, because the lens has done the job.

The key to effective preaching is to discover the central truth that a Bible passage contains. Indeed, whether we preach from a verse, a passage, a chapter or a Bible book, we will always want to focus on its primary message. Books on preaching use various images to convey this: What is the *big idea* of this passage? What is the main *theme*? In the case of a Bible book as well as a passage, what is its *melodic line*? What is the *heartbeat* of the section?

Our work in explaining and applying the passage will mean that every other aspect of our message will be committed to pressing home that dominant thought. Some writers express it quite simply: they refer to it as the 'Aha!' of the passage, the 'Aha!' of the sermon, which at least implies the sense of excitement about the discovery. 'Yes – this is what it is all about!' Or, as the disciples on the road to Emmaus declared, 'Were not our hearts burning within us . . . ?' (Luke 24:32).

In fact, Charles Simeon described this priority with characteristic directness:

> Reduce your text to a simple proposition, and lay that down as the warp; and then make use of the text itself as the woof; illustrating the main idea by the various terms in which it is contained. Screw the word into the minds of your hearers. A screw is the strongest of all mechanical powers . . . when it has been turned a few times, scarcely any power can pull it out.[1]

This dominant thought will be the key issue on which we will wish to focus. It will determine the thrust of our message, around which everything else will revolve. It is often said that preaching is different from a lecture, not least because of its commitment to hammering home that one idea. Preaching will be effective if, by the Spirit's presence and empowering, we gather all aspects of our message to help the congregation grasp this theme and sense its power. Listeners need this focused emphasis. Remember, 'it is easier to catch a baseball than a handful of sand'.[2]

Selecting a passage

In chapter 1, we saw the enormous value of preaching from a Bible passage. This ensures that we are drawing from one primary unit of thought and focusing on that one theme. Now, selecting a passage, or planning a preaching programme, is a big subject, and we will only touch on it here. There was a time when preachers began their sermon with 'a text', which usually meant one Bible verse, and although that might be sufficient for an exposition if, for example, it is a focused statement in one of Paul's letters, it is not always an appropriate way to preach, because a verse (even a Pauline one) needs to be seen in its wider context, and set within the thought unit which the author is developing. An isolated verse can all too easily become the peg on which we hang our own thoughts (remember?), rather than provide the dominant thought intended by the author. This is why a paragraph or passage is usually the best unit, since it is long enough to establish the author's intention and theme.

Many churches aim for consecutive exposition, preaching through sections of a Bible book. That has become the norm for the preaching at Keswick Convention too. This has great advantages, allowing a congregation to capture the book's melodic line, understand its context and benefit from the continuity. When carefully planned, it can also provide a balanced diet of Old Testament, Gospels and epistles, modelled on Paul's concern 'to proclaim to you the whole will of God' (Acts 20:27). There is also a place for teaching larger sections of the Bible, such as one sermon for each of the twelve Minor Prophets, helping a congregation to understand the broad sweep of biblical truth. Where we need to address topics or themes, a different preaching style will be needed, although a primary Bible passage can still be very helpful. And for those in churches that use a lectionary, with two or three passages provided for each Sunday, there is wisdom in selecting just one of the options provided, enabling the preacher to speak with both clarity and focus.

In essence, then, we are seeking to press home the dominant theme which the author, inspired by the Spirit, has provided for us in the passage. This helps provide the focus a preacher needs, while also guiding the congregation in how to use Scripture. As Alan Stibbs wrote,

> The preacher's example may influence them to read it for themselves with increased faith, zeal and satisfaction, because they have experienced under the preacher's ministry how God can use the written Word and its careful and prayerful study to give light and understanding, encouragement and hope.[3]

The journey from text to sermon

Many people have been helped by an illustration devised by Ramesh Richard, encouraging preachers to look first at the *flesh* of the passage (surface details, ideas, words, illustrations), then to press beneath the surface to discover the *skeleton* (framework, structure or flow of thought), and then to discover the *heartbeat* – the key idea which is pumping the blood around, the life-giving force of this passage of Scripture. The diagram on the opposite page outlines these ideas. (It is also reproduced in Appendix 4.)

One of the most valuable ideas in this model relates to discovering the heartbeat. The model is based on a simple journey from bottom left, up and over the bridge, and down to the bottom right. Here's a summary:

We begin by studying the *meat* of the text. That is, we examine the surface details: sentences, words, pictures and paragraphs. We chew over the text, absorb it, meditate on it, think about it. Through this process, we are understanding the context and the details of the passage, as we saw in the last chapter, becoming familiar with its taste and feel.

Next we come to the *bones*. That is, as we study a passage, we begin to identify a possible outline structure, its skeleton, those things that provide its shape and make it hold together.

From text to sermon

Bible passage: _____

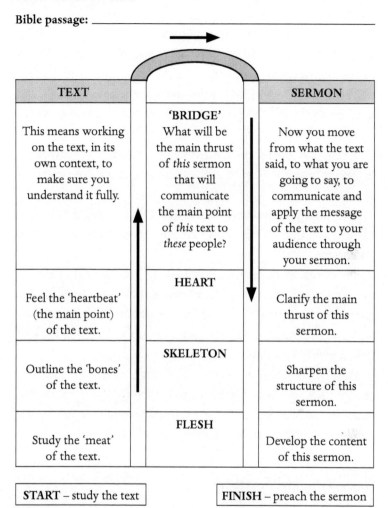

TEXT	'BRIDGE'	SERMON
This means working on the text, in its own context, to make sure you understand it fully.	What will be the main thrust of *this* sermon that will communicate the main point of *this* text to *these* people?	Now you move from what the text said, to what you are going to say, to communicate and apply the message of the text to your audience through your sermon.
Feel the 'heartbeat' (the main point) of the text.	**HEART**	Clarify the main thrust of this sermon.
Outline the 'bones' of the text.	**SKELETON**	Sharpen the structure of this sermon.
Study the 'meat' of the text.	**FLESH**	Develop the content of this sermon.

START – study the text   **FINISH** – preach the sermon

[Adapted from Ramesh Richard, Scripture sculpture method. Used with permission.][4]

It is then that we move to the *heartbeat*, as we ask ourselves: what makes this text live? What is it that is pumping the blood around; what is the passage so passionate about? What is the point, the main theme? We need to be able to express this in a simple sentence. It should not be a selection of ideas, but the big point.

Then, as you see from the diagram, we cross over the *bridge* at the top. In doing so, we ask: what will be the main thrust of *this* sermon that will communicate the main point of *that* text to *these* people? Having discovered the heartbeat, I must now be faithful in explaining that theme to the particular audience to whom I must preach.

Then, having established that heartbeat, we work *back* down the right-hand side of the diagram, as we now craft the sermon.

We clarify the *heartbeat* – the main thrust of the sermon, the theme that needs to be clearly brought home to the audience.

Then, we work on the *skeleton* – the outline structure for the sermon, the shape of the message. Here, we look for the ideas that support the heartbeat, that hold the message together, enabling it to flow appropriately. (We will look at this in more detail in the next chapter.)

Finally, we come to the *flesh* of the sermon. This is the content that is needed in order to clothe the skeleton. Some discipline is needed here to ensure there is not too much content and that it truly sticks to the skeleton.

Discovering the heartbeat

Our purpose will not surprise you. It is to ensure that the listener hears the heartbeat of the sermon. Indeed, this should really become the preacher's heartbeat too, as we carry this message in our hearts and minds, and convey the message to others. We are the 'echo-chamber' of the text: it should resonate within us as we work on the passage and then deliver its message.

As this model implies, if we are to communicate the meaning of a passage to our congregation, it is essential first to have discovered the heartbeat, the main theme that will dominate our message. Speaking personally, discovering the intended purpose and significance of the passage is the most important part of my preparation. Unless I am clear about this, I will not be able to preach with conviction and passion. I will be offering generalizations or clichés or a jumble of reflections, but not the incisive Word of the Lord.

We are the 'echo-chamber' of the text: it should resonate within us as we work on the passage and then deliver its message.

This is central. As we have already seen, Bible exposition does not mean that every sermon has to be 'exegetical', working verse by verse as if we are providing an audio commentary. Exposition can take many culturally different forms and should also be appropriate to the literary genre of the text itself. It is in fact exposing the fundamental meaning of the passage, opening up its force and power, showing people how it applies to them, and urging them to accept and respond to it.

But how do we identify the focus within a Bible passage? Again, the literature on this theme is extensive, but I will highlight three foundational ideas:

Context: we first follow the disciplines of 'understanding' (already seen in chapter 3). We aim to comprehend the situation of the writer and his first listeners. This is essential if we are to be true to 'what God said to them then'.

Principle: we must then determine if there is a general principle embodied in this passage which can be applied in all contexts. What is the meaning which stands above culture and context and which represents the primary theme for each generation?

Implication: we then craft our message to reflect how that principle is applied in our specific culture and context.

A word for today

Now, I am well aware that I am making some big assumptions and am in danger of oversimplifying complex processes. But, if I am a preacher, this rule of thumb will help me to discover the message that needs to be expressed to my audience.

Let's take a well-known passage from 2 Corinthians: the account of Paul's thorn in the flesh in chapter 12, verses 1–10. First, it's clear from the whole letter that Paul is being criticized by a group of so-called super-apostles who doubted his credentials as a leader. They expected strength, not weakness; they looked for a commanding presence, not physical vulnerability; they wanted impressive rhetoric, not simple preaching. So, in chapter 11, Paul prepares his CV – an extraordinary catalogue of sufferings. His critics were big on boasting, and so he decides to boast as well, but to boast about his weaknesses. For sure, he could recall a remarkable spiritual experience many years ago, but since that was in danger of generating pride, he realized that the Lord had given him a thorn in the flesh to keep him from becoming conceited (12:7). But what was it? We don't actually know. Quite a few people have made suggestions, but it is good that Paul didn't declare what it was, for reasons that will become clear. He had repeatedly asked the Lord to remove it, but that hadn't happened. Instead, the Lord spoke to him about its purpose: 'My grace is sufficient for you, for my power is made perfect in weakness' (12:9). And Paul realized that now he really could 'boast' – he *would* boast – about his weaknesses, so that Christ's power would rest on him. As we think about discovering the main theme here, it's probably now becoming clear. So, this is the sequence of study.

> The *context* is one of pressure, from his critics, from the catalogue of suffering in his ministry, as well as from the overwhelming pain of the 'thorn'. The context also includes first-century views of what makes a leader (not too different from our own culture, in fact).

> The *principle* is clear, because the Lord's reply was not specific to the exact suffering or to the thorn itself: it was an assurance of power made perfect in *weakness*.

> The *implications* follow: I can guarantee that there is not a congregation in the world where this message – the 'heartbeat' of God's grace being made perfect in our weakness – does not resonate, irrespective of the culture or situation.

Preaching this passage means keeping that heartbeat right at the centre. Preachers need to avoid being distracted from that primary purpose, whether by debating what Paul's ecstatic experience might have been, or what the 'third heaven' was (12:1–4), or the exact nature of the thorn (12:7), or how it could have been a 'messenger from Satan' (12:7), or what it means that he prayed 'three times' (12:8). Depending on the situation and where we are preaching, some of these issues might need to be explained. But we must never lose sight of what is pumping the blood around this passage and, indeed, around the whole 2 Corinthians letter. 'My grace is sufficient for you, for my power is made perfect in weakness' is a profoundly encouraging implication for all hard-pressed believers. And that illustrates why preaching must be focused.

In the previous chapter, we worked on the closing doxology of Habakkuk's prophecy (Habakkuk 3:16–19), seeking to understand its context and examine the details of the verses. We used a simple grid to explore this (also reproduced in Appendix 2). That study is exactly the same as the study process on the left-hand side of the Ramesh Richard diagram which we met earlier in this chapter (and in Appendix 4). In other words, we have worked hard to examine the *flesh* (the words, sentences, images) of the passage, then the *bones or skeleton* (the flow of thought or, in the case of Habakkuk's doxology, the change of mood), and then its *heartbeat*.

We can also look at Habakkuk 3:16–19 following the sequence of *'context-principle-implications'*, as we seek to focus on the core message. The *context* is the terror of the Babylonian invasion, the destruction of Jerusalem (with all of its devastating economic and social consequences) and Habakkuk's new awareness of God's purposes. The *principle* we draw from the passage is that, despite the turmoil of our world, God's people can trust God's purposes. And the *implications* become clear: whatever our personal circumstances, or whatever might be happening in the global world order, God is ultimately in control – we can entrust our lives and futures to him.

The pastoral preaching of such a passage will have greater resonance and more profound implications if the preacher has understood its context, looked carefully at the way Habakkuk wrote his song, and focused the message around Habakkuk's own heartbeat. In the next chapter, we will look at how that message can be presented in a compelling and memorable way. But first, an important word about how a clear focus can also be reinforced through the simple means of a strong introduction and conclusion.

The beginning and the end

I often aim to introduce a sermon by means of a contemporary illustration that resonates with my audience, one which clearly highlights the big idea or heartbeat of the message. This is an attempt to make the connection (an issue we will explore in chapter 6), but also to build a bridge with my audience as I introduce the dominant theme or the sermon focus. And the same is true of a conclusion. I have always appreciated the advice given to me many years ago, that it is best to write out a short conclusion, clearly summarizing the main focus of the message and, having explained this, to stop! Sometimes, we hear preachers who have trouble landing. I once flew into Entebbe in bad weather, and as the plane made its approach, it almost touched down, but then suddenly swept up into the air once again. This happened two or three times as the pilot made sure that the landing would be safe. Some preachers have a tendency to do the same: they think they are coming in to land – but no, off they go once again for another few minutes, adding to the congregation's bewilderment or discomfort or both. Preaching with focus will mean a helpful introduction and a short conclusion, both of which affirm the main theme. Then, we can all land safely and the message can find its place in our hearts, minds and lives.

On my wall at home, I have some prints of photos delivered by my Nikon lens. A little pretentious perhaps, but the sharply focused puffin on the island of Staffa, or the pensive mood of my daughter's face, bring back a wealth of memories – sights, smells, people, events. One clearly focused image recounts a substantial narrative. And so it is with preaching too: a focused message, founded on the timeless truth of a Scripture passage, grips my heart. Such messages live in my memory, active and dynamic, continuing their work. Because of the faithfulness of preachers whom I have heard, life-changing words have been screwed into my mind so that nothing can remove them.

•

5

Biblical preaching must be clear

One Sunday, at the close of the service, a confused congregation member spoke to the preacher at the door. She
explained to him that his sermon reminded her of the peace
of God, as Paul described it in Philippians 4:7, 'which tran-
scends all understanding'! I'm afraid that sometimes there is
indeed a fair amount of fog in the pulpit. Some preachers
leave their hearers less clear after the sermon than they were
before it.

We have seen that Ezra and his team worked hard to ensure
the reading of the Scriptures was clear, something that
doubtless involved translation, explanation and discussion.
We too will help our listeners better understand what we are
saying if we are clear in the way in which we present our
message. Some form of structure is nearly always helpful,
whether that be the clear plot-line of a Bible story, the stanzas
of the poetry in a psalm, a series of questions addressed to
the text to bring out what it is saying, an emphasis on one
theme approached from different angles, or a progressive
building of the biblical argument (maybe even with three

points!) – but always with a sustained emphasis on the main theme or heartbeat of the passage. So, there are many different ways of shaping a sermon, but some kind of structure is important.

The advantage of the simple model we used in chapter 4 – flesh, skeleton and heart – is that it encourages clarity in both theme and structure. We have already seen why a clear focus is essential. In the same way, a clear outline or structure will help everyone too. And there are some important issues to remember.

Three things about an outline

First, *an outline must be true to the passage.* Since our exposition must open up the passage and handle that with integrity, any outline must arise from the passage itself and not be imposed from outside. However striking or creative our headings might be, if they do not represent the content, then we are failing in our task of honouring the authority and primacy of the Word. One key issue in Bible exposition is to preach it according to its given form, to go with the flow of the literary genre. For example, we must allow a Bible story to do its work, not flatten it by reducing it to isolated teaching points. Similarly, as one writer has expressed it, we must allow 'a parable to surprise us, a lament to move us, a prophet to shake us, a proverb to provoke us and the Gospels to convict us'. In that sense, we not only seek to preach the main theme of a passage, but also aim to do this in a way consistent with the form of literature we are expounding. David Day makes a helpful observation: 'A preacher who ignores the literary form of the passage is like a cook who takes an already existing cake and breaks it up in order to use the crumbs as ingredients for a totally different dish.'[1]

Secondly, *a clear structure can help listener and preacher alike*. It helps listeners in several important ways, for example, allowing us to see the significance of the text. It keeps us focused on the themes of the Bible passage, the source of preaching's authority. If, as listeners, we are drawn back to the main ideas of the Bible passage, that will reinforce the fact that this is what truly matters. Also, it often helps us listeners to concentrate. Whatever we believe about attention spans, it is usually the case that following through step by step is a good way to show the listener where the preacher is heading and how he is getting there. And, in turn, it can help us to remember the passage and perhaps its outline, as long as it is not artificial and does not distort the message of Scripture.

A preacher once spoke to the Christian student group at Yale in the US. He decided to use the letters of Y-A-L-E to define his four sermon headings. It turned out to be such a long four-point sermon that one student commented afterwards that he was glad he was not studying at the M-A-S-S-A-C-H-U-S-E-T-T-S I-N-S-T-I-T-U-T-E O-F T-E-C-H-N-O-L-O-G-Y. Best to keep it simple.

Clear outlines also help the preacher. As we have seen, working on a Bible passage to examine the flesh, skeleton and heartbeat makes for careful preparation. We ensure that we are working hard at what the text says, what its flow of thought might be, and how to communicate that effectively. Then, when we come to preach, a simple outline can also guide our preaching, ensuring that we stay true to the main message and how that is developed, providing the shape for what we want to say. If we are quite new to the task of preaching, an outline will also allow us to time our sermon properly and emphasize the main points in adequate ways.

Thirdly, *there should be rich variety in the way an outline can be constructed*. Much has been written about the value, but also the predictability, of three points! We need first and foremost to be true to what the passage itself offers up, rather than imposing a one-size-fits-all structure on every part of the Bible. Sometimes, a sermon can be formulated by a question and a series of answers. Sometimes, I have heard preachers in Africa emphasize the main point, circling round to punch it home again, and then circling round once more, to press the theme still harder, all without obvious structure, but with clear flow and intention. For many of us, there might be a simple and memorable sequence of related headings. But whatever structure we adopt, there are several principles to bear in mind.[2]

Unity: the various sections must clearly hold together, unified around the main message of the sermon.

Harmony: the sections reflect the theme of the passage, but they possibly also echo one another in a way that is memorable or forceful. There should be a progression to an appropriate culmination in the message.

Simplicity: there should not be too many sections or subsections, but an appropriate shape that arises from the passage, with each section given due weight and each expressed with simplicity.

Putting flesh on the bones

In seeking to preach with clarity, I offer one final tool (also reproduced in Appendix 5). It is a simple sheet of paper which allows the preacher to ensure that he is being true to the flow of thought and structure of the message, addressing issues in a manner that will help clarify the thrust of the sermon. Speaking personally, I sometimes have this sheet on my desk as I reach my final stages of preparation. I know this simple paper has its dangers: it could lead me to think I must always have the 'divinely inspired' three points, for example. But that's not the intention. Whatever structure we deploy (and we have seen the different ways in which that can be done), a simple device for checking that we are covering the ground in an accessible and timely way may be worth using. We are all different, and I offer this as it may well be as useful to others as it has been to me.

At the head of the sheet of paper (see p. 104), I will first summarize the 'heartbeat' of the passage, the main point of my message. Every other aspect of the message connects with that, as spokes to a hub. The heartbeat should also shape the manner of my introduction and conclusion.

The paper has the chosen structure or outline along the top, reflecting how we are to handle the Bible passage. On the left-hand side, there are five areas to consider in our preparation:

1. *What is the link between each point and the main theme or heartbeat?* Does each section of our outline serve the purpose of clarifying the thrust of the message? This is vital, since it provides the unity.
2. *Are there issues in each section that might need explaining?* This is a valuable question to ask during preparation, because it helps us to be selective about what we include and exclude. Are there issues that the congregation really does need to know about, or questions they will surely be asking? And are there details here which we can lay aside, which we can reference but not develop?
3. *Are there other supporting Bible references that we need to include?* Again, a word of caution. Our main task is to explain this primary passage and not complicate a

Bible passage: _____

Heartbeat: _____

Verses:	Section 1	Section 2	Section 3
What is the link with the main theme?			
What must I explain?			
What other Bible references should I use?			
What examples could I give?			
What application should I bring?			

message with a string of other references. But very often, it is necessary to speak of what has gone before this passage, or to set it into context. And often there are significant passages to which we must refer, such as when an Old Testament passage needs a New Testament connection, or where the central theme of our passage is qualified or helpfully developed elsewhere. We might need a few well-chosen references, but not too many.

4. *Are there good examples I can give?* We all know when an example or illustration serves to shed light on the Bible's teaching in a memorable way, and again, the art of preaching is to select sufficient illustrations to serve exactly the purpose of that section of Scripture, bringing it home to our life or culture, and strengthening the congregation's understanding of its implications.

5. *What specific application can I bring?* The best application is woven throughout the message rather than in the final two minutes, and our simple paper allows us to think of appropriate areas where application can be pressed home at each stage of the sermon's development.

Since, in chapters 3 and 4, we dipped into Habakkuk's prophecy at various stages, we will complete that journey by looking at how we might structure a message from the remarkable doxology in Habakkuk 3:16–19. Earlier, we established the flow of thought – the skeleton – of this short passage, marked by the change of mood. We saw how the verses moved from the trembling and the waiting of verse 16 to the rejoicing of verse 18, through to the more confident mood of verse 19. And we also noted how all three ideas related to Habakkuk's trust in God, the God for whom he will wait (verse 16), the God in whom he will rejoice (verse 18), and the God by whom he will be strengthened (verse 19).

Then, in chapter 4, we focused on the theme, that Habakkuk and all of God's faithful people can trust God's purposes, whatever their circumstances.

As I prepared a sermon around that theme, I looked for a simple way of structuring a message that would reinforce that core idea – the heartbeat – whilst also providing clarity through a memorable outline. Under the title of 'Trusting the Lord in difficult times', I selected the following:

Rest in the Lord   3:16
Rejoice in the Lord   3:17–18
Rely on the Lord   3:19

In this way, I sought to ensure the sequence was true to the passage – always the first rule. Next, I checked that each heading related clearly to the main theme of trusting the Lord – this is a God-centred passage, and so repeating that emphasis reinforces that theme. Then, I used the simple device of parallelism as a way of creating a memorable sequence and rhythm, deploying words that reflect the structure of the song – rest, rejoice, rely. We all know how this approach can be overplayed, with an artificial alliteration that evokes a wry smile on the faces of the congregation. That's why we have stressed in this chapter that there are many other ways to create the needed clarity. Creativity is very important, sustaining an element of surprise and provoking a congregation to think freshly about a passage. But my choice of these three headings was an attempt to capture the key elements of Habakkuk's song which can be taken to heart by God's people in any context or culture.

Finally, I sought to fill out the simple grid in this chapter by checking each stage that it outlines:

- the link between each of my three points and the main heartbeat of the sermon;
- verses that might need explaining (the reason for Habakkuk's trembling; the 'nation invading us'; the devastation of verse 17 – as we saw earlier);
- supporting Bible references (I used them sparingly, selecting only 2 Corinthians 4:7–12 and Romans 8:28, 35–39 in order to build the bridge to the work of Christ and its implications for Christian living);

- a careful use of both examples and illustrations that
  would connect with my audience.

In these ways, as the passage found its place in my mind and
heart, I hope it also brought home to my listeners the
life-changing truth that our lives, our families, our nation,
this world and the entire universe are held in the hands of
the Sovereign Lord who will surely bring about his good
purposes.

Clear communication

Last, but not least, a word about clarity in the way we speak.
We will see in the next chapter that Peter and Paul chose
their words carefully according to their audience. If we are
going to make the meaning of the Bible passage clear, then
we too have to use words that are clear and that, as far as
possible, everybody in the congregation will understand.
There is no need to fill a sermon with long theological words
or critical concepts dredged up from a textbook or commentary. We should use the ordinary language of ordinary
people, with illustrations and applications drawn from their
everyday lives. Often, this can make a huge difference,
opening the curtains so that light is shed on the meaning of
the passage.

Depending on our context, it is often helpful to provide
an outline for the congregation, whether on the printed
service sheet or on the screen. This can have its dangers,
but a simple and well-presented outline will provide visual
clues that many people appreciate, allowing them to follow
the text and its message, and sometimes commit it to
memory. The reason for working hard at a clear theme,
clear structure and clear communication is exactly the

same as it was for Ezra's team of helpers who 'read from the book of the Law of God, making it clear and giving the meaning so that the people understood what was being read' (Nehemiah 8:7–8).

6

Biblical preaching must be relevant

One Saturday morning, I was working in my office when I heard voices on the street two floors below. I looked out and saw a group of Christians preaching in the open air. It was the main street, with heavy traffic and the crunching sound of buses changing gear, but the group lined up and, one by one, stepped forward, shouting at the cars and the occasional shoppers.

I watched them with mixed emotions. On the one hand, here were my fellow believers who were brave enough to preach the gospel boldly in our city. On the other hand, it was very poor communication indeed. A wide gulf separated them from their audience. They used a version of the English Bible that was hundreds of years old; they could hardly be heard; and people kept their heads down as they walked past – there was no interest, no eye contact, only embarrassment.

The teachers and preachers in Scripture had a God-given calling to deliver God's message to a particular people – a word that in the first instance was for a particular context and which addressed a particular need. And the prophets, the apostles and Jesus himself are all wonderful examples of people who made the connection, bringing God's Word to a contemporary audience. The message was not delivered with detachment or cool professionalism, nor without regard as to whether or not the listeners heard or understood.

We have seen this clearly from Nehemiah 8. The Word was opened in the streets of Jerusalem, and every effort was made to ensure that everyone could see and hear and, in particular, understand. Using groups of helpers to translate and explain the message, every adult and every child was to hear and understand. We too need to make the text of the Bible accessible, engaging not only with Scripture, but with our listeners. As we saw in the last chapter, we present God's Word in a clear way that can be grasped, but we must also do so in ways that resonate with their situation.

We must build bridges between the world of the Bible and the world of today.

Our point in this chapter is a simple one: as preachers prepare to preach, they must spend time not only thinking about what they are preaching about, but also thinking about whom they are preaching to. Sadly, there is often what one writer has called 'a plague of dullness' in some people's preaching, usually as a result of not being sufficiently thoughtful about the needs of our audience, nor sufficiently creative in the way we capture their interest. We must build bridges between the world of the Bible and the world of today.

The Word that works

To recap, the primary focus is the faithful explanation of God's Word. The Bible must be central, and the preacher must immerse himself in the text and work hard to explain its message. The Word of God sets the agenda; the Word does the talking. It is not a matter of 'trying to make the Bible relevant'. This authoritative and powerful Word will speak directly to every age and culture, since its author is God the Creator and Redeemer, the One who reshapes worldviews and reorientates broken lives. There is nothing more relevant than God's Word. And, as we work hard to discover its focused message, we know that it will be incisive: 'For the word of God is alive and active. Sharper than any double-edged sword, it penetrates even to dividing soul and spirit, joints and marrow; it judges the thoughts and attitudes of the heart' (Hebrews 4:12). This is because the Holy Spirit is working through the Word, convicting, applying, comforting and encouraging. We can be sure that the Word will do the work. Darrell Johnson is right when, writing about the issue of 'implication and application' in preaching, he stresses, 'God's Word not only informs the listener, leaving the listener to perform it; God's Word performs, working on and in the listener.'[1] He goes on to quote the key verse that I highlighted earlier: 'the word of God, which is indeed at work in you who believe' (1 Thessalonians 2:13).

So, what is our responsibility, if we are preachers, as we seek to ensure that the Word of the Lord speaks to today's generation? I can think of five things.

Truth that transforms

The preacher is not a lecturer delivering information. You may know this definition of lecturing: 'information being passed from the notes of the lecturer to the notes of the student, without going through the minds of either'. It is obviously a fundamental issue of integrity that preachers are themselves being shaped by the power of Scripture. We are handling God's dynamic Word, which must first become a part of us, bearing fruit in our lives, challenging our value system, our lifestyle, our attitude to sin and temptation, and the realities of our day-to-day living. We will have nothing to communicate if we have not encountered that truth for ourselves. We need to get inside the text, and the text needs to get inside us. Our audience will soon notice if the message is having its impact on us.

Perhaps this is the fundamental issue in bridging the gap between the world of the Bible and the world of our day: our lives as well as our lips communicate the message. I remember having to speak in my home church one Sunday on John 11 and the story of the raising of Lazarus, which confronts us with the issues of life, death and resurrection. It happened that the day before, early on the Saturday morning, my father died. I was confronted immediately with the need not just to rehearse the biblical truth of the difference Jesus makes in the face of death, but to believe and live that reality. It had to be true in my life at that very moment, and not simply something I had read about in a Bible commentary.

An essential part of this process – of our getting inside the text and the text getting inside us – is that the truth of the Word must increasingly shape our understanding of the world. A biblical worldview helps us more truly to analyse the needs of the world in which we live and the context into which we must speak that authoritative Word. How are we to understand our world? The first answer is that we have to understand our Bibles, to have a biblical worldview. If we are to understand what is happening in our culture, we can do so only as we understand the big themes of the Bible – the storyline which ranges across the story of creation, fall, redemption and new creation. This has to be our framework for viewing the whole of life.

I do all I can to watch the cultural trends, reading papers and magazines about social issues or politics or religious belief. But so much of the analysis that we read in the media is superficial. It might be serious academic reflection on the part of sociologists or psychologists, and this certainly has significant value, but it does not take into account the real nature of our human condition, nor the opportunities and hopes of God's gracious interventions through Christ. By contrast, the Word of God will mould our thinking, clarify our perspective and provide the framework by which we can properly interpret what is happening in the world around us. Commenting on the story of Jeremiah, Eugene Peterson makes a wise observation: 'If we forget that the newspapers are footnotes to Scripture and not the other way round, we will finally be afraid to get out of bed in the morning. The meaning of the world is most accurately given to us by God's Word.'[2]

Preaching that connects

Whilst never losing sight of the priority and centrality of the Word, we must not miss the dialogical value of going from Word to world and from world to Word. There is a necessary two-way conversation between God's Word and the rest of life. Many years ago, I spoke with a university student who explained, 'If I think about my subject as a Christian, I'll be in terrible trouble.' So she decided it was best to keep these two parts of her life in separate compartments. And this mindset is surprisingly common amongst Christians generally. It is as if the Bible is kept in quarantine. No two-way conversation exists between it and our lives. We don't bring the questions of life to the Bible, and we don't allow the challenges of the Bible to be brought to our lives. So, our task in preaching is to do all we can to overcome this, first as it becomes relevant and life-transforming for us, but also as we seek to do all we can to understand what is happening in our world.

Sometimes, we Christians are accused of displaying an ostrich mentality, as if our faith effectively removes us from the real world. On a recent TV quiz show, *University Challenge*, one of the teams represented a British theological college. They were able to answer most of the questions on philosophy and religion with commendable accuracy, but they failed miserably when it came to the questions on popular culture. The response of the quiz-master, Jeremy Paxman, was: 'You need to get out more', and that's not bad advice to theological students who are called to minister in the contemporary world.

One important aspect of this responsibility is to assess the mood of our culture, to understand the big issues and the commonly expressed questions, the things that are finding their way into newspapers and magazines or TV chat shows, issues that are causing anxiety or shaping the popular consciousness. It's worth reflecting on what these might be and discussing them with others. For example, there is a great deal of uncertainty about the world order just now. Even ordinary people, not usually given to thinking about ultimate issues or big political ideas, are impacted emotionally by what's going on: terrorism, rogue states, the challenges of Middle East instability, all of which provoke a fundamental sense of insecurity. *What exactly is going on in our world?*

Many similar questions surface in a conversation with friends in the pub or families in our street. And it's not simply: what's happening in our world? but: *who can I trust?* The decline in confidence in the political process, in religious or business leadership, fed by the economic collapse and political corruption, all cause people to wonder who can be relied upon? Then there are the demanding moral questions of our age, including those associated with gender and sexuality or end-of-life issues. Many of our friends have lost their bearings and have no clear moral framework for assessing what is right and what is wrong. *How do I make decisions?* In many parts of the world, young people are pessimistic about their government, their social and economic future, the possibility of employment and any likelihood of long-term stable relationships. Social commentators tell us that this generation of young people is more anxious, more uncertain about the future, than recent generations. This is the first generation of young people in a century to have fewer high hopes than their parents. *Exactly what does the future hold?*

Or what of the issue of spirituality? We know that the idea of the secular West is a myth, as issues of religion and spirituality still remain in the popular consciousness. But people are very confused, typified by the oft-quoted remarks by the former English cricket captain, Mike Gatting: 'I believe in a bit of everything – God, the supernatural, ghosts, superstitions, UFOs. I like to keep my options open.' *What am I to believe, and does it really matter anyway?*

There is much more that could be said here, but each of these questions exposes the vulnerabilities of our culture, providing an important access point for God's Word to make its powerful impact, for God's Spirit to convict of sin, righteousness and judgment, and for God's Son – Jesus himself – to meet the anxious parent, the self-sufficient businessman, the despairing student, the confused child.

Preachers who identify

There is a further step that preachers must take. We must understand the world, but we must also feel its pain. This is a demanding, but essential, aspect of speaking the truth to the people of our day. It means getting under their skin, feeling their sorrows, identifying with their needs. It was supremely true of Jesus. The Word became flesh – a first-century Palestinian Jew, a tradesman in humble circumstances, a compassionate but incisive teacher who felt the pains and sorrows of the people to whom he ministered.

The prophets demonstrated the same commitment, called to identify with their listeners. I have often been moved by the example of Jeremiah who, for forty years, was God's lonely opposition spokesperson. He had a hugely demanding job, proclaiming God's message of judgment and restoration. It was an uncomfortable calling – he is sometimes called 'the life and soul of the funeral'. But his ministry impacted him deeply. His preaching was not delivered from a distance, but spoken with tears in his eyes. You can sense the desperation in his prophecy:

> The harvest is past,
>> the summer has ended,
>> and we are not saved . . .
> Is there no balm in Gilead?
>> Is there no physician there?
> (Jeremiah 8:20, 22)

He knew that the people to whom he was speaking – his people – were suffering from a terminal illness. He was nursing a dying patient: 'The harvest is past . . . and we are not saved.'

Ezra is a key player in the Nehemiah 8 story, and it is worth remembering that he was not simply an academic scholar, aloof from the challenges of the people he addressed. Later in Nehemiah's memoirs, we read that Ezra and Nehemiah confront a major sin in the life of the people – intermarriage

with women who practised pagan idolatry (Nehemiah 9 and
10). Nehemiah confronted the people head-on (Nehemiah
13:25), but Ezra followed the example of Jeremiah. Seeing the
people's faithless response, he tore his clothes, sat in mourning,
and included himself as he confessed their sin. He identified
with those whom he taught, and wept because of their sin
(Ezra 9:6, 15). And it was this which provoked repentance as
the people followed Ezra's dramatic example: 'While Ezra was
praying and confessing, weeping and throwing himself down
before the house of God, a large crowd of Israelites – men,
women and children – gathered round him. They too wept
bitterly' (Ezra 10:1).

To enter this broken world, to feel its sorrows, to engage
with its struggles, to fear its judgment, to hope for its redemption in Christ – this transforms the way we speak the truth.

Steven Covey highlights the importance of such identification with a personal story of his journey one morning on
the New York subway. The occupants of a carriage were
quietly reading their Sunday papers, when a man and his
children boarded. The children were shouting, bouncing off
the seats, grabbing people's newspapers, but the father sat
with his eyes shut, doing nothing. Everyone felt irritated, not
only by the children's behaviour, but by the man's apparent
insensitivity. 'So finally, with what I thought was unusual
patience and restraint, I turned to him and said, "Sir, your
children are really disturbing a lot of people. I wonder if you
couldn't control them a little more?" The man lifted his
gaze . . . and said softly, "Oh, you're right. I guess I should do
something about it. We just came from the hospital where
their mother died about an hour ago. I don't know what to
think, and I guess they don't know how to handle it either."'
Steven Covey described how everything changed in an instant
– he saw things differently, thought differently and behaved

differently. His heart was filled with the man's pain, and this changed how he saw the man, the children and the needed response.[3]

It was said of the British TV newsreader, Trevor Macdonald, that after delivering the news to the nation, he would often be found weeping in his dressing room, profoundly moved by the painful message he had had to deliver. Jeremiah knew the same:

> *Preachers don't speak down to people; they draw alongside them.*

Since my people are crushed, I am crushed;
   I mourn and horror grips me.
(Jeremiah 8:21)

We are 'dying men speaking to dying men'. Preachers don't speak down to people; they draw alongside them. As David Day has expressed it, 'If asked where does the preacher stand, we need to say, "Like Christ, down in the Jordan with everyone else."'

Preaching with faithfulness and relevance

When I was younger, involved in a church in London, the work of evangelism presupposed that most unbelievers at least knew that the Bible began with God, that he was the Creator, that the Bible had two Testaments, that Christmas was to do with Jesus' birth and that Easter was to do with Jesus' death. And so our churches and our evangelists could speak about sin, the cross, repentance and faith. Christian language and a biblical worldview weren't central to the culture, but they were familiar to most people. As we sought to explain the Christian faith, we had some obvious common ground. Now, however, it is entirely different. We meet many who have no idea who Jesus was, and who certainly don't know how he died. Biblical stories and Christian language are becoming foreign to our culture.

The sermons in the book of Acts are well-known examples of how the apostles were faithful to the truth but relevant to their audience. It is worth highlighting the example of Peter's sermon in Acts 2 and Paul's sermon in Acts 17. Peter preached to a Jewish audience, and, as has often been pointed out, the message was constructed in such a way as to reflect the background and interests of his congregation. He could cite the Old Testament because the audience was thoroughly familiar with it; the Scriptures were an authority that they recognized and were committed to. And similarly, he used language which they understood – explicitly theological language about Jesus as Lord and Messiah, the long-awaited deliverer, Jesus as the fulfilment of Israel's expectations and longings (Acts 2:16–28).

Paul spoke in a very different context when he preached in Athens. He spoke to people without a biblical worldview, who lived in an environment dominated by secular Greek paganism. Their language, their authorities, their worldview were quite unlike those of the audience in Acts 2, and so Paul spoke quite differently from Peter. His message was much more comprehensive, ranging across the nature of the universe, the reality and nature of God, the issues of human history and anthropology, human identity, destiny and accountability. He knew that without that wider picture, the description of Jesus and his work would make little sense. He aimed to set out a biblical worldview, into which the central theme of Jesus Christ fitted (Acts 17:22–31).

So too in our day. We are living in our confused religious, post-Christian, biblically illiterate culture. We must enter and understand this world in order to speak to it. Our calling is to speak with faithfulness to God's eternal Word and with relevance to our contemporary audience.

Entrusting the outcome to God

When I was in my teens, I did my best to persuade my school friends that the Christian faith mattered. Most days, I walked to school with a good friend who argued persuasively against the Christian position. He was much brighter than me, and I lost most of the arguments. The discussions went on for several years, until we eventually left school. He had not become a Christian. He went to university, and within a matter of weeks, I received a letter from him, explaining that he had wandered into a meeting hosted by the Christian Union and had committed his life to Christ. My first reaction on reading the news was to think, 'That's so unfair! After all of those years of discussion!' But of course, what a great answer to prayer and what great evidence, as I soon realized, that the work really is the Lord's.

We must not minimize the strenuous effort involved in understanding the world in which we live, identifying with its needs, building the bridges for effective communication, devoting time to deepening friendships, formulating our apologetics, and living the gospel with integrity and authenticity. It will take everything we have. But we must remember that it is the Word which does the work. I often recall the wonderful promise made through Isaiah:

> As the rain and the snow
>   come down from heaven,
> and do not return to it
>   without watering the earth

and making it bud and flourish,
    so that it yields seed for the sower and bread for the eater,
so is my word that goes out from my mouth:
    it will not return to me empty,
but will accomplish what I desire
    and achieve the purpose for which I sent it.
(Isaiah 55:10–11)

Preaching that Word will never be a waste of time.

7

Biblical preaching must be embodied

The American evangelist D. L. Moody once said that every Bible should be bound with shoe leather: we are to walk in the ways of the Lord. The truth is not simply something to be believed; the truth is to be 'done'. In today's world, the demand for authenticity and integrity means that no preacher is worth listening to whose own life does not demonstrate the truth about which he preaches.

Climbing the wooden tower specially constructed for him, Ezra took centre stage in the dramatic events in Jerusalem that day. Nehemiah made sure that the scholar-teacher carried the responsibility of opening the Word. Ezra came from a long line of priests, and he too had been living in exile with God's people. But whilst he had been living in a pagan culture dominated by idolatry, hundreds of miles from Jerusalem and the temple, he had been faithfully studying God's Word and teaching its laws to God's people in Babylon. Finally, he was granted permission to return home to Jerusalem – 'the gracious hand of his God was on him' (Ezra 7:8–9). And it is no surprise that he played a central role in calling the nation back to the Word. What made him such a remarkable figure in the Nehemiah 8 story is summed up in a pithy statement found in Ezra 7:10: 'For Ezra had devoted himself to the study and observance of the Law of the LORD, and to teaching its decrees and laws in Israel.'

The one dominant verb – 'devoted' – describes his commitment to three things, conveyed by the secondary verbs: study, observe, teach. He had set his heart and mind fully to that essential sequence. Derek Kidner suggests that the secret of his lasting influence was that 'what he taught he had first lived, and what he lived he had first made sure of in the Scriptures'.[1] In case we should imagine that preachers, teachers and scholars must devote themselves simply to study and to teach, the Scriptures underline the central importance of *doing* the truth, of obeying, living, embodying that Word. What Ezra taught, *he had first lived*. Indeed, here is an important key to effective teaching and true godly scholarship. As Michael Wilcock once expressed it, our understanding of God's Word has to do with our obedience and not just our brains. True understanding arises from living the truth, not just believing the truth. And here we come to a fundamental aspect of the dynamics of biblical preaching: *the Word must be embodied* in the life of the preacher.

When Joshua embarked on his challenging new career as the leader of God's people, he was given these instructions: 'Keep this Book of the Law always on your lips; meditate on it day and night, so that you may be careful to do everything written in it. Then you will be prosperous and successful' (Joshua 1:8). The sequence is here once again: regular nourishment from God's Word, careful thinking about its implications and a firm intention to obey all that God has revealed.

We know how much this matters in our churches and in our culture, but we are also acutely aware of our failures in Christian community, most painfully seen amongst pastors and preachers. The late Dallas Willard tells the story of a pastor who became very angry at something that was done during a Sunday morning service. Immediately after the service, he found the person responsible and gave him a merciless rebuke. Unfortunately, he was still wearing his (live) radio microphone, and his angry exchange was broadcast over the entire church building – in all the Sunday school rooms and even in the car park. 'Soon afterwards he moved to another church,' Willard comments.

We know how often this type of thing happens. As I have engaged in seminars in different continents over the years, the comments have always been the same. In Hong Kong, I was told that Chinese pastors preach well, but behave terribly at home; in Africa, most countries appeal that any training event for pastors must include a session on being a godly husband and acting faithfully in marriage and family life; and in Asia? Here is what one wife wrote: 'I would like to know more about Langham Preaching, because not only does my husband preach better, he is a much nicer person.' ☺

I have written elsewhere about why such consistency and integrity are essential in all Christian ministry, and have often felt that if we are preachers, we not only need to heed the usual advice of practising what we preach, but perhaps we should only *preach what we practise*. I realize that to do this will drastically reduce the length and variety of my sermons, but surely it is at the heart of integrity, and essential for the authentic preaching of God's Word?[2]

Paul was also acutely aware of the danger facing Christian leaders. The pastoral epistles offer guidance on the profile of leaders, emphasizing significant aspects of personal behaviour and character which are essential qualities for leading the church (1 Timothy 3:1–13; 4:6–16; 6:3–6, 11–16; 2 Timothy

2:14–26; 3:10–17; Titus 1:6–9; 2:1–15; 3:8). Paul spoke person-ally to Timothy about the need to 'set an example for the believers in speech, in conduct, in love, in faith and in purity' (1 Timothy 4:12). He urged Timothy, 'Watch your life and doctrine closely. Persevere in them, because if you do, you will save both yourself and your hearers' (1 Timothy 4:16). And Paul could also appeal to his own life as evidence that he embodied the Word. As he said to the Ephesian elders in his moving farewell address, 'You know how I lived the whole time I was with you, from the first day I came into the province of Asia' (Acts 20:18). And, as he did with Timothy, he urged them, 'Keep watch over yourselves . . .' (Acts 20:28). Watch your own life, your behaviour, your spiritual well-being.

To trace the significance of this theme, I offer three prin-ciples taken from Paul's first letter to the Thessalonians.

Three important principles

1. *The gospel must be embodied*
Early in his letter, Paul describes how the gospel came to the Thessalonians, and this is a good definition of integrated preaching: 'Our gospel came to you not simply with words but also with power, with the Holy Spirit and deep con-viction. You know how we lived among you for your sake' (1 Thessalonians 1:5). Paul's description of the preaching task was certainly not restricted to communicating information. He adds three other expressions: proclaimed in God's power, proclaimed with full conviction and proclaimed with the Holy Spirit who empowered the preacher and pressed home the truth to the hearer. But there is a further phrase in verse 5 which is closely connected to the rest of the verse. Our gospel came to you with power, so 'you know how we lived among you for your sake'.

In fact, on several occasions, he encourages them to remember 'how we lived'. The gospel that he proclaimed was also bearing fruit in his own life, and it was this combination which made his gospel communication so effective: God's Word, proclaimed in the power of the Spirit and embodied in the messenger himself. And this is to be expected. The truth of the gospel is dynamic and life-changing. God's Word 'is indeed at work in you who believe' (1 Thessalonians 2:13). It is truth that produces godliness, as Paul said to Titus, and this is no more significant than in the life of the herald, the one who proclaims that truth.

> *Authentic preaching is when Word, Spirit and life combine.*

This was exactly the burden of Jeremiah as he called the prophets of his day to be consistent in word and life. Not only had there been an appalling theological deterioration, but also deep-set moral failure amongst the prophets. Instead of leading people away from sin, the prophets actually confirmed people in such activity: 'they live a lie,' he said. A true prophet will be one whose own life is an embodiment of the truth, part of his message. As David Day expresses it, 'He is not like a postman who can do what he likes in private as long as he goes on delivering letters.'[3] Authentic preaching is when Word, Spirit and life combine.

This embodiment can be seen in the remarkable way in which Paul identified with the Thessalonian believers, which is a further essential feature of the life of the preacher:

> As apostles of Christ we could have asserted our authority. Instead, we were like young children among you. Just as a nursing mother cares for her children, so we cared for you.

> Because we loved you so much, we were delighted to share
> with you not only the gospel of God but our lives as well.
> (1 Thessalonians 2:6–8)

He describes his unreserved commitment to them, not only working hard to support himself, but constantly giving himself to others.

This is all the more important in a postmodern culture which has become weary or cynical about words. Authenticity in Christian ministry demands that our lives embody our message, and if the gospel describes God's power in the apparent weakness of Jesus on the cross, our ministry will follow that same pattern of costly identification. Colin Morris describes such authentic preaching in his book, *The Word and the Words*: 'It is not from a pulpit but a cross that power-filled words are spoken. Sermons need to be seen as well as heard to be effectual. Eloquence, homiletical skills, biblical knowledge are not enough. Anguish, pain, engagement, sweat and blood punctuate the stated truths to which men will listen.'[4]

2. The preacher must be approved

Next, Paul highlights that he was called by God to carry out this ministry: 'We speak as those approved by God to be entrusted with the gospel' (1 Thessalonians 2:4). Part of the context of the letter is Paul's attempt to reply to his critics who claimed he was not a true apostle. So, he explains in direct terms that his ministry arose from being commissioned by God. God had approved him and sent him, and he now felt a deep sense of responsibility because, as a steward, he had been entrusted with the gospel. The word 'approved' includes the idea that God had tested Paul. Through his life and ministry, through his catalogue of sufferings, God was approving him for this apostolic ministry. It is fair to conclude that Paul's passion for proclaiming the gospel, and his ability to rise above criticism and opposition, arose from this deep sense of testing and calling.

Such a calling for today's preachers will not simply be a letter from a mission agency or selection by a candidates' committee: it will be a testing in our lives, a forging within our character and inner being of a proper adult godliness that makes us fit for the ministry to which God has called us. It is only then that we can speak honestly about our motivation. 'We are not trying to please people but God, who tests our hearts. You know we never used flattery, nor did we put on a mask to cover up greed – God is our witness. We were not looking for praise from people, not from you or anyone else' (1 Thessalonians 2:4–6). Once again, this is part of Paul's reply to his critics. He was charged with error, impurity, deceit, flattery, insincerity and self-seeking (verses 3, 5). One great advantage of criticism is that it forces you to test your fundamental motivations. For Paul, it was clear: 'We are not trying to please people but God' (verse 4); 'We were not looking for praise from people' (verse 6). There were no mixed motives. He was transparently honest. There was no insincerity, no deceit, no self-seeking, but everything was above board: 'You know . . . God is our witness' (verse 5); 'You are witnesses, and so is God' (verse 10).

All Christian ministry, as Paul has demonstrated, is costly. But there is always a severe temptation – particularly if God grants you a measure of success – to become self-seeking, for your motives to become distorted and for your ministry to lose integrity. This is especially the case for those frequently found in pulpits, welcoming the adulation of the crowd. We constantly face the insidious enemy of Christian ministry. Eugene Peterson nails it:

Any Christian is at risk in any of the temptations. But those of us who do work explicitly defined as Christian – pastors, teachers, missionaries, chaplains – live in an especially hazardous environment, for the very nature of the work is a constant temptation to sin. The sin is, to put an old word on it, pride. But it is often nearly impossible to identify pride, especially in its early stages. It looks and feels like energetic commitment, sacrificial zeal, selfless devotion . . . We become Christians because we are convinced that we need a Saviour. But the minute we enter into a life of ministry we set about acting on behalf of the Saviour.[5]

This can lead to a kind of professionalism that separates personal life and public ministry. We become arrogant, spiritually dry and exhausted, as we try to live two lives. Preachers must first preach to themselves. They must allow God's Word and God's Spirit to transform their lives, as they refocus on the significance of their calling – to study, yes; to teach, yes; but first and foremost, to obey.

3. Ministry must be modelled

Charles Simeon was concerned about integrity: 'No amount of homiletical technique can compensate for the absence of a close personal walk with God. Unless he puts a new song in our mouth, even the most polished sermons will lack the sparkle of authenticity.'[6] It was because of Paul's commitment to embody the truth that he could appeal to the Thessalonians to follow his example. That really is preaching with authenticity! 'You are witnesses, and so is God, of how holy, righteous and blameless we were among you who believed. For you know that we dealt with each of you as a father deals with his own children, encouraging, comforting and urging you to live lives worthy of God, who calls you into his kingdom and glory' (1 Thessalonians 2:10–12). Paul piles up the adjectives in verse 10 in a dramatic way – 'holy, righteous and blameless'. This was at the heart of his ministry. And godly example can be an enormously influential ingredient in a healthy church. As we often comment, Christian character is as much caught as taught. So Paul could say to the Corinthians, 'Follow my example, as I follow the example of Christ' (1 Corinthians 11:1). This was also why he was so concerned to avoid the opposite influence: 'We put no stumbling-block in anyone's path, so that our ministry will not be discredited. Rather, as servants of God we commend ourselves in every way' (2 Corinthians 6:3–4).

In 1 Thessalonians 2, Paul is reinforcing the point that there was nothing in his life or lifestyle which could be made an excuse by others for not believing God's gospel. His message and his ministry were wedded to a godly life that made the gospel credible and believable. And not only that. Paul states in verses 11 and 12 that this also shaped his pastoral ministry. Like a father, he encouraged these believers 'to live lives worthy of God', to follow his example. It was for this reason that Richard Baxter urged pastors and preachers: 'We must study as hard to live well as how to preach well.' It is of vital importance that preachers ensure their lives are truly modelling the truth of the gospel, and that, like a parent, they are giving energy to the shaping and forming of other disciples, through encouragement that is supported by practical and genuine example.

The first chapter of 1 Thessalonians contains a final example of the power of embodying the Word. It is a sequence, or a chain reaction:

Verse 5   the gospel came to you
Verse 6   you welcomed the message
Verse 8   it rang out from you everywhere

And the same ripple effect is described in terms of modelling and emulating:

Verse 6   you became imitators of us
Verse 7   you became a model to all the believers in
           Macedonia

From the seaport of Thessalonica, the message rippled out, echoing around the mountains, spreading far and wide. And it was not just a message, but a model. People heard about the impact of the gospel on the church. It had an effect not only on surrounding cities and provinces, but across time and generations: 'Your faith in God has become known everywhere' (1:8). That ripple effect still works wherever the Word is faithfully lived and proclaimed, which is why our own commitment to experience the transforming effect of that Word is so important. John Owen was right when he insisted that 'if the word do not dwell with power *in* us, it will not pass with power *from* us'.[7] This is a fundamental issue of authenticity in preaching and integrity in the church. The gospel must be embodied.

So far, we have looked at *the Word of God and the heart of preaching* and have seen that biblical preaching must be *centred on God's Word*, must *pray God's Word*, and must *understand God's Word*. Next, we looked at *the teacher and the work of preaching*. We saw that biblical preaching must be *focused*, must be *relevant*, must be *clear* and *embodied*. This brings us to the third main element of the story in Nehemiah 8. It is not simply the story of Ezra the teacher, but a dramatic account of the multi-layered response of God's people. Since the Word was being read and explained, and since that Word was dynamic and powerful, it inevitably had an effect. Something was happening to the hearers.

Warm-up

'Imagine an impatient audience at a rock concert picking up the chant: "We want Ezra, we want Ezra", saying it over and over, louder and louder, and you get some idea of the feelings being expressed.'[1] Jim Packer made this intriguing suggestion as he thought about the crowd gathering in the city centre in Jerusalem that day. They were eager to hear the Word. In fact, it was the people themselves who had taken the initiative and called on Ezra to bring out the Book (Nehemiah 8:1).

Preaching is not simply to do with the preacher – their study and then their delivery. All preaching must be especially concerned that the Word finds its home in the heart, mind and will of the hearer.

So, what was happening with the assembled congregation in Nehemiah 8?

They were expectant

The sense of eagerness and expectancy is expressed in verses 3, 5 and 13, where we find that the people were attentive to the reading, that they stood up when it began, and that they devoted time to studying it together. This reminds us of Luke's comment about the Bereans who, after Paul had preached to them, 'received the message with great eagerness and examined the Scriptures every day to see if what Paul said was true' (Acts 17:11). And it reminds us too that there is little to be gained from reading the Bible without such expectancy. Jesus' own ministry was frustrated when there was no expectancy on the part of his hearers, when he began to teach in the synagogue and was met with cynicism and incredulity (Luke 4:24–30). Expectant faith is the soil in which God's Word will bear fruit.

'Ezra praised the LORD, the great God; and all the people lifted their hands and responded, "Amen! Amen!" Then they bowed down and worshipped the LORD with their faces to the ground' (Nehemiah 8:6). We all have something to learn from the attitude of the people in Jerusalem that day: a longing for God to speak as they lifted up their hands and, with reverence and respect, bowed with their faces to the ground. These too may well be prerequisites to understanding God's Word and coming into his presence. For of course, the people were not idolatrously worshipping the book itself, but the God whose voice they were listening to through it. Indeed, the verse is important in reminding us that we don't venerate the Bible as such: its purpose is to bring us into the presence of its author, the Lord, the great God.

So, Nehemiah 8 demonstrates the vital element in true preaching: it should bring us into God's presence. As Jim Packer once expressed it:

The joy of Bible study is not the fun of collecting esoteric titbits about Gog and Magog, Tubal Cain and Methuselah, Bible numerics and the beast, and so on; nor is it the pleasure, intense for the tidy minded, of analysing our translated text into preacher's pretty patterns, with neatly numbered headings held together by apt alliteration's artful aid. Rather, it is the deep contentment that comes from communing with the living Lord into whose presence the Bible takes us – a joy which only His own true disciples know.[2]

Preaching mediates an encounter not merely with the truth, but with God himself.

A further sign of their spiritual hunger was their seriousness. They were ready to cope with all kinds of inconveniences in order to hear this Word. They stood there at the Water Gate from daybreak to noon (verse 3) – for at least five hours, without a coffee break in sight – because they longed to hear and understand what God had to say to them. For sure, this response of commitment was to do with God's Spirit. There are many things that we will need to do to make God's Word accessible and understandable, as we have already stressed. But more than anything else, we need the Holy Spirit to make people serious in their longing to hear and respond to it.

They were obedient

The people responded to the Word in several significant ways. We see their initial response in verse 9: 'For all the people had been weeping as they listened to the words of the Law.' So, their first hearing of the law provoked within them a sense of contrition as they realized that their lives had failed to match up to the standards which God had set. But intriguingly, Ezra and Nehemiah move quickly to set that failure within the wider context of God's purposes for his people. With the encouragement of the leaders, the people went on to celebrate, to eat and drink 'with great joy' (verse 12). They had come to realize that it was God's desire to bless them, something they had discovered from all that had been read: 'They now understood the words that had been made known to them' (verse 12). And so, the effect of God's Word was not only that the people wept out of contrition, but also rejoiced at God's grace. Good preaching should have the same double effect today.

The rest of chapters 8 and 9 demonstrate the impact of the Word on the people. First of all, we see that on the second day, when they rediscovered the law concerning the feast of booths, and realized that it was the date when they ought to be celebrating it, they went out and did so (8:14–17). The point here is not the exact details of what they did, but that, as soon as they understood what God's Word said, and how it applied there and then, they went out and obeyed it. Their study of the law was strongly intentional. And we should note in passing that Nehemiah records for a second time that there was great rejoicing (verse 17), joy when they understood God's Word (verse 12), and joy when they obeyed it (verse 17). Isn't that the kind of joy we should seek in our churches, through faithful preaching producing obedience?

Then, in Nehemiah 9, the people put their intended obedience on a firm basis. They held a great ceremony of covenant renewal, which concluded with the solemn words: 'In view of all this, we are making a binding agreement, putting it in writing, and our leaders, our Levites and our priests are affixing their seals to it' (9:38). This was an expression of their commitment to obey God's Word. Later, they claim that they had bound themselves with 'a curse and an oath to follow the Law of God given through Moses the servant of God and to obey carefully all the commands, regulations and decrees of the LORD our Lord' (10:29).

So, they were ready for action. They wanted to live their lives in conformity with God's Word, to demonstrate in their community that they belonged to him. That's the significance of the sequence of these chapters: hearing God's Word, celebrating God's goodness, knowing God's grace and then obeying God's laws. Here is truth in action. As we have already seen, truth is dynamic and life-changing: we are called to *do* the truth, not simply to believe it. And that's the purpose of preaching – to lead to determined faithfulness.

As we learn from the congregation in Jerusalem that day, we draw several lessons for today's churches: biblical preaching must *involve the congregation*, must *be applied*, must *depend on the Spirit* and must *proclaim God's grace in Christ*.

8

Biblical preaching must involve the congregation

Have you noticed how certain forms of music naturally draw the listener in? Toes begin to tap, heads start to nod, and the listeners begin to hum along. Composer and musician know what they are doing: by repeating certain musical phrases or improvising to a jazz riff of repeated chords, the audience not only begins to listen, but becomes part of the experience. This is true not only with jazz or rock, but also with classical music.

An *ostinato* is a musical theme that is repeated or gradually developed, but in such a way as to capture the listener. It can be found in African music, a Baroque suite or in boogie-woogie jazz. It has a magnetic quality, helping the listener to engage more and more as the music develops.

That's what we long for with preaching. The congregation not only hears, but truly engages – heart, mind and soul – actively becoming part of the experience. This is partly achieved through the careful crafting of a biblical message, emphasizing the main theme and repeating its refrain. But mostly, it happens in the wider context of receiving that Word in God's presence and among God's people.

How does the Nehemiah 8 story compare with your experience of a church service? We live in entirely different worlds and contexts, of course, but I'm thinking of how the people at the Water Gate engaged with the reading of the book of the law. For many contemporary Christian congregations, the sermon can be the part of the service when we are most passive. I have mentioned that surveys indicate that the majority of church attendees long to hear the Word of the Lord. But often we have surprisingly low expectations of engagement, and perhaps this is one reason why we are sometimes disappointed by the preaching event. We are simply observers. It's the time to settle back for twenty minutes, wondering how the speaker will do. We might assess his performance, but we don't really see ourselves as active participants.

The ingredients that make up the Nehemiah 8 story reveal a very different dynamic. The congregation longs to hear that Word, pleading with Ezra to bring out the book. They are willing to stand for hours as they listen carefully. They respond actively by bowing to the ground or lifting their hands. And significantly, the reading of the law is complemented by smaller gatherings for explanation and discussion. Then, add on their active obedience to what they had heard and understood, as they celebrated the long-neglected feast of tabernacles by joyfully eating and drinking, or subsequently built their booths as part of the religious festivity – 'as it is written' (Nehemiah 8:15). Then, they returned once again to hear the Word being read and explained, day after day, from the first day of the feast to the last (Nehemiah 8:18). This congregation was anything but passive!

What if our church congregations were similarly engaged? Of course, a Sunday morning service in Jarrow is a far cry from a seven-day feast in the streets of Jerusalem. But it still begs the question: longing to hear God's Word, willing to give generous proportions of time, responding to the message with repentance, confession, thanksgiving and worship, discussing its implications, going out in obedience? The expected outcome, as one writer suggested in a provocatively ambiguous phrase, is that preaching should drive people from the church! The preached Word must so capture hearts and minds and wills that it is embodied and enacted in the world. Preaching must be a community event for precisely this reason. Let's explore some of these dimensions.

God's presence with his people

We begin by recognizing the special significance of gathering as the church. Just as our expectations of preaching might be limited, so too can be our expectations of the corporate life of the church. But we should recall the simple promise of the Lord Jesus: 'Where two or three gather in my name, there am I with them' (Matthew 18:20). We will shortly see that Christ is the theme of biblical preaching, but his promise in this passage reminds us of his *presence* when believers gather to hear that Word. In a demanding chapter about church discipline in Corinth, Paul uses a telling phrase regarding the church assembled in the name of the Lord Jesus: 'the power of our Lord Jesus is present' (1 Corinthians 5:4). He makes the same point later in the letter when he tackles the place of prophecy and tongues in congregational worship: the unbeliever entering the Christian community will 'fall down and worship God, exclaiming, "God is really among you!"' (1 Corinthians 14:25).

In an exceptionally helpful booklet on this theme, William Philip underlines the need for active participation by every member of the congregation when God's Word is preached.

> A proper corporate focus also liberates us from the wholly mistaken notion that the rest of the congregation are passive in the process of preaching, merely recipients of Bible teaching, accruing knowledge and information, but not otherwise involved. We can see that nothing could be further from the truth, if we consider what is happening in terms of such a real encounter and engagement with God. Together we draw near to God, as he draws near to us through the means of his Word.[1]

As we see from the letter to the Hebrews, meeting *one another* is not an end in itself. The goal is always meeting one another in order to draw near to meet with *God himself.*

Whilst there is some value in downloading mp3s of famous preachers or listening to messages online, this can never be a substitute for hearing the Word preached in God's presence and amongst his people. That's the context for biblical preaching, where Word, Spirit and congregation combine.

God's gifts for his people

It's obvious of course that preaching must be a corporate event, unless the preacher is practising in front of the mirror. The whole point of the gifts from the ascended Christ which Paul describes in Ephesians 4 is that they are entirely community-centred, 'to equip his people for works of service, so that the body of Christ may be built up until we all reach unity in the faith and in the knowledge of the Son of God and become mature, attaining to the whole measure of the fullness of Christ' (see Ephesians 4:7–13). So, we don't focus exclusively on the one called to teach, but on God's purpose for the whole congregation, to whom he has given his Word and for whom he has given the gift of teaching. And whilst acknowledging the role of the pastor-teacher in the congregation, we should never elevate their ministry inappropriately, since all gifts are given for the building up of the congregation and for the glory of God, not to build personal reputations or feed personal egos. In fact, Scripture demonstrates that every believer is called to the ministry of the Word in the local church: 'Let the message of Christ dwell among you richly as you teach and admonish one another with all wisdom . . .' (Colossians 3:16).

God's people at work

We saw that the Jerusalem congregation in Nehemiah 8 was fully engaged as the Word was read and explained. How can every believer play their part when the Bible is preached? There are three big responsibilities:

1. Active listening

Jesus was particularly insistent that his audience should truly hear what he was saying: 'Whoever has ears to hear, let them hear.' That seems to have been one of his characteristic sayings (Mark 4:9, 23; Luke 8:8), and some writers liken this frequent command to the way Israel's daily creed opens: 'Hear, O Israel' (Deuteronomy 6:4). But hearers need help. Good listening means we will have responsibilities before, during and after the sermon. Before the sermon, preachers need to find ways to stimulate congregations to be praying and expecting to hear what God has to say through his Word. Wherever possible, we should give some introduction to the passage on which we will preach. If we have planned a series over several weeks, then we should encourage people to read the passage in advance. During the sermon, we must urge listeners to engage with the passage for themselves. One of my daughters enjoyed being part of a congregation for several years where the pastor, Mark Ashton, became known for a particular phrase during his preaching: 'Look at your Bibles!' This is very good advice, encouraging everyone to honour the Bible's authority and seek its message. Certainly, if at all possible, we should encourage people to have a Bible open in front of them as we preach. In an age when the Bible passage can be displayed on the main screen at the flick of a switch, I would still encourage churches to resist projection at this point, and aim to keep everyone physically handling the Bible itself, whether a print version or an electronic tablet. Finding the passage, checking the verses, seeing the context, assessing the meaning, checking the preaching – all are significant disciplines to be nurtured.

Whatever level of ability our congregation has in reading, we should encourage such disciplines as expecting, focusing, memorizing, discussing, praying and applying. In other words, people don't settle back in their seats at sermon time, assessing the performance of the speaker. We learn from the response of God's people throughout Scripture – expecting an encounter with God, ready to respond to his Word and open to being changed by its power. We have seen that preaching should be a dynamic and a divine event. As Luther said, 'I just threw the Bible into the congregation and the Word did the work.'[2] Or as Tom Wright has expressed it: 'Preaching is meant to be an occasion when, so to speak, God happens.'[3]

In describing the Puritan vision of the Christian life, Jim Packer highlights some significant lessons for preaching, one of which relates to the energetic engagement of the congregation:

> They taught their congregations to memorize the sermons they heard, looking up references, taking notes if need be, so

that they could 'repeat' the messages afterwards and meditate on them during the week. The ministry of the Word was thus a cooperative activity, in which the laity were to labour to learn just as hard as the minister laboured to teach.[4]

Describing the variety of listening styles that might be found in a typical congregation, Michael Quicke once gave his listeners some challenges, including listening with all your mind, heart, soul and strength. He encourages us to question and interact with the sermon's points and flow:

> Though the average person speaks at a rate of 125 to 150 words per minute, the average person can listen at a rate of 500 words per minute, a difference that allows the mind to wander . . . Improving concentration involves focusing on the speaker, following the words, anticipating the next point, and testing what has been said so far.[5]

Many churches help us by providing an outline on the service sheet with space for making notes, or even pausing during the sermon to allow time for quiet reflection or a brief discussion or corporate prayer. Jesus was entirely realistic when he suggested in the parable of the sower that we all have issues in our lives that interfere with our response to the Word (Luke 8:1–15). So, we must do all we can, in practical ways as well as in spiritual preparation, to create favourable conditions – good soil – for receiving the Word. Neither should the preacher underestimate what we have addressed in chapter 7 – the necessity of the preacher embodying the Word. This is because our willingness as a congregation to listen will depend to a great extent on our capacity to trust the preacher. A preacher's inconsistent living extinguishes our respectful listening.

Recent writers on preaching have devoted attention to the importance of *learning*, not just teaching. There are indeed several simple actions that we can take to reinforce our learning and enhance our response. Preachers can help in the way they present their material, an issue we have touched on several times. One obvious way is to dialogue, just as Paul did in his writing and preaching. I know that some suggest that this is hardly engaging the congregation, but many of us have experienced the value of this kind of provocation. Paul frequently pushed his listeners: 'Do you not know that your bodies are members of Christ himself?' (1 Corinthians 6:15); 'Do you not realise that Christ Jesus is in you?' (2 Corinthians 13:5); 'You were running a good race. Who cut in on you to keep you from obeying the truth?' (Galatians 5:7).

A preacher's inconsistent living extinguishes our respectful listening.

Then, some time for reflection is important, something that begs for church services to be constructed in such a way as to allow for quiet after the preaching. For others, discussing the Word over a simple lunch, perhaps interrogating the speaker, but certainly engaging with the Bible passage and with fellow believers, can make all the difference in grappling with the Word and its implications. (See Appendix 7 for some questions to use in evaluating a sermon.) Then, some churches deliberately link the Sunday preaching with the weeknight home-group discussion – not always easy, but a valuable reinforcement of the teaching if the church programme allows for this.

It is well worth making available a booklet on listening to sermons. *Listen Up!* by Christopher Ash, for example, contains some valuable encouragements, and realistically includes advice on how to listen to bad sermons too.[6]

2. Prayerful expectancy

The Jerusalem congregation certainly longed to hear the Word, and we know that the vast majority of churchgoers look forward to the sermon too, hoping for direction or encouragement or challenge. Prayerful expectancy is indeed an essential partner to faithful preaching. By definition, preaching is a community event that brings corporate responsibilities, not least the necessity of our urgent appeal to the Lord to speak. And we can be certain that he will respond to such a prayer: 'Call to me and I will answer you' (Jeremiah 33:3).

The Lord's invitation to the thirsty given through Isaiah is a beautiful passage for our prayerful engagement as we come to hear the preacher.

> Come, all you who are thirsty,
>   come to the waters;
> and you who have no money,
>   come, buy and eat!
> Come, buy wine and milk
>   without money and without cost . . .
> Listen, listen to me, and eat what is good,
>   and you will delight in the richest of fare.
> Give ear and come to me;
>   listen, that you may live . . .
> Seek the LORD while he may be found;
>   call on him while he is near.
> (Isaiah 55:1–6)

William Philip says that in the New Testament corporate prayer is intimately linked to the ministry of the Word so as to be inseparable from it, and he quotes from Ephesians 6 to make this clear: 'Take . . . the sword of the Spirit, which is the word of God, praying at all times in the Spirit, with all prayer and supplication' (Ephesians 6:17–18 ESV). How much more God could do in our lives and our churches if we were to engage with his Word through active listening and prayerful expectancy!

3. Determined obedience

Preaching should drive people from the church (in the right sense!), as we've suggested. All preaching should call for change, as we will see in the next chapter. Without this element, preaching lacks its distinctive purpose. But the listener must listen in a truly Christian way – with a firm purpose to obey. We have seen the sequence in Nehemiah 8 and 9, as the people heard God's Word, celebrated God's goodness and obeyed God's commands. We have seen how Ezra was committed not only to study and teach the law, but to obey it. To make a commitment to obey means that I am making the Bible passage my own, hearing the Word, welcoming it in as a friend, allowing the seed to enter the soil and produce a harvest. James could not have been clearer: 'Do not merely listen to the word, and so deceive yourselves. Do what it says' (James 1:22).

We should do likewise.

9

Biblical preaching must be applied

The art of preaching is application, suggests Alec Motyer, and we can understand why. Surveys suggest that the vast majority of Christians attending a church service long to hear a word from the Lord that will change their lives. We are hungry for the nourishment of the Word, eager to see it shape our families and our church, often desperate to know the pathway we should walk and how to access the resources we will need. We want to see the Word at work. Ezra and Nehemiah opened the Word of God not simply as a religious exercise, a duty to fulfil now that the walls were built. They saw it as the new constitution for the people of God, and knew that it was essential to shape their lives, their families, their economic activity, their relationships and their community.

We saw in chapter 6 that the Word of God does not need to be 'made relevant'. Faithfully and clearly explained, it speaks to every aspect of our human condition. And we should expect this: God's Word does its work. Scripture not only says things; it does things. As pastor-theologian Peter Adam has stressed, the New Testament's most important claim about itself is that it is effective. So, when our preaching is rooted in the Bible and energized by the Spirit, it has the capacity to transform lives, families and communities. The aim of preaching is to make God's Word clear so that, by the Holy Spirit, people understand it in their own situation and then obey it. All preaching must be transformational preaching, provoking the listener to consider and then to act.

We know that Jesus left no room for neutrality or boredom when he preached. And in his record of various sermons preached in the book of Acts, Luke often describes how the people reacted, not with passivity, but with joyful acceptance, or alarm, or amazement, or even antagonism. Preaching seeks to change lives. As Paul said about the Romans: 'But thanks be to God that . . . you have come to obey from your heart the pattern of teaching that has now claimed your allegiance' (Romans 6:17).

We could, then, insist that the preacher's task is only to proclaim the Word; it is the work of God's Spirit to apply the truth and transform the listener. Yet, we should not dismiss our responsibility too quickly. As John Stott pointed out many years ago, the doctrines of incarnation and inspiration demonstrate God's concern to address humankind through specific languages and cultural contexts. These were highly particularized events.[1] In the same way, our concern must be that that same Word should enter the particular contexts of our day and generation. This in no way lessens our commitment or conviction regarding the power of that Word. But the big concern in Nehemiah 8 is also that of all biblical preaching – to ensure that the Word is truly understood. Our task must include a determination by God's Spirit to facilitate that too. As Bryan Chapell expresses it, 'Without the "so what?" we preach to a "who cares?"'.[2] Our concern is that the Word finds its place in the hearts and minds of our hearers, and so I will comment on three themes regarding its application. The first concerns the nature of Scripture, the second the role of the congregation, and the third the responsibility of the preacher.

The purpose of preaching

The most well-known description of the purpose of Scripture is found in Paul's writing to Timothy: 'All Scripture is God-breathed and is useful for teaching, rebuking, correcting and training in righteousness, so that the servant of God may be thoroughly equipped for every good work' (2 Timothy 3:16–17). God's intention is to change us, and so preaching those Scriptures is to open up the passage in such a way that its message is clear and its implications for change obvious.

Paul demonstrated this in his guidance to Titus. He not only encouraged him to teach in line with apostolic doctrine (Titus 2:1), but went on to outline exactly what that would look like:

> Teach the older men to be temperate, worthy of respect, self-controlled, and sound in faith, in love and in endurance. Likewise, teach the older women to be reverent in the way they live, not to be slanderers or addicted to much wine, but to teach what is good. Then they can urge the younger women to love their husbands and children, to be self-controlled and pure, to be busy at home, to be kind, and to be subject to their husbands, so that no one will malign the word of God. Similarly, encourage the young men to be self-controlled.
> (Titus 2:2–6)

Of course, looking at these life-instructions which were spoken in the first century, preachers and congregations will need prayerfully to do more to assess their implications for the Christian life in a different century and a different culture. But the point is clear: teaching is set in the context of careful exposition, doctrinal fidelity *and* practical exhortation.

James has much to say about this, of course. His writing expresses the wisdom found throughout the Scriptures – knowing how to live God's way in God's world. The Bible is not interested in knowledge that stays in the head. Indeed, one might even say that we don't really 'know' anything until we have put it into practice. James makes the connection between the truth of the Word and the need to live integrated, ordered, godly lives. Three times in chapter 1, he warns us of the danger of self-deception: 'Don't be deceived . . .' (1:16); 'Do not merely listen to the word, and so deceive yourselves. Do what it says' (1:22); 'Those who consider themselves religious and yet do not keep a tight rein on their tongues deceive themselves, and their religion is worthless' (1:26). So, how can we avoid being deceived? How can we walk wisely in a godless world full of trial and temptation? By listening to and obeying the Word. In chapter 1 there are three references to the truth:

It doesn't take too much imagination to see how the Bible connects with our lives.

'He chose to give us birth through the word of truth' (1:18); 'Get rid of all moral filth . . . and humbly accept the word planted in you' (1:21); 'Do not merely listen to the word . . . do what it says' (1:22).

This is incredibly practical. It doesn't take too much imagination to see how the Bible connects with our lives. Dale Ralph Davies makes the point that if a preacher has a lively sense of his own depravity, he won't have much trouble applying Scripture! 'Use your sinful nature to good advantage,' he suggests. 'You will apply the Word of God in its narrative form much more potently . . . and graciously.'[3] The point here is that part of our task in explaining the Bible will mean making the connections with everyday life, showing how it impacts on our daily walk. Psalm 119 repeatedly affirms,

> I gain understanding from your precepts;
>> therefore I hate every wrong path.
> Your word is a lamp for my feet,
>> a light on my path.
> (Psalm 119:104–105)

The congregation at work

In chapter 6, we saw the necessity of both understanding the Word and understanding the world. This was referred to by John Stott as 'double-listening'. Mark Greene proposed an additional ingredient in the mix when he wrote about the 'three-eared preacher', someone who listens to the Word and the world, but also listens carefully to the congregation. This makes the job of preaching a community activity, as we have seen. This additional ear is important. Paying careful attention to those to whom we speak is something we assume to be central to the task of pastoral care or counselling, and the same disciplines of listening and observing must be true for the preacher too.

It was said of John Wesley that he worked hard to understand the needs of his congregation, sitting where they sat in the literal sense of entering the church building before the Sunday service and assessing how his message might be heard and received by different people. Another practice advocated by some preachers is to write the names of people we know who will hear this message on our preparatory notes, as a visual trigger to help us call to mind their needs. In fact, this should perhaps naturally become part of our 'praying the Word', which we looked at in chapter 2. As we meditate on its truth, we will reflect on its implications for our own lives first, as well as for the lives of our fellow believers. This requires not only our reason, but also our imagination and emotions.

This is simply another way of restating that we must share the gospel and our own lives as well. The more 'professional' we become, the more distant we become. With our fellow believers, we recognize our shared need of God's grace. As D. T. Niles said about the task of evangelism, it is one beggar telling another beggar where to find bread. So, in all preaching, it is essential that there is authenticity. Perhaps there are things we need to learn about voice projection or eye contact or finding the right pace of delivery. But what matters most of all is not being artificial or preachy, but truly being ourselves, expressing our personality, our humanity, our need of God's grace.

Applying God's Word is the responsibility of all of God's people. In the last chapter, we saw that whenever the Bible is preached, everyone is engaged. Just as in Jerusalem, today's congregation must be listening, assessing, reflecting, discussing, applying and obeying. We know we need to find ways to make that happen, but more than anything else, it is a matter of conviction about the significance of the Word. What is the agent for change in this broken world? What is it that will introduce the kingdom and produce truly lasting transformation, that radical deliverance for which people long? Jesus gives the answer: 'The seed is the word of God' (Luke 8:11). If the metaphor of the seed reminds us of apparent vulnerability, of weakness, of slow growth, then it also reminds us of another truth – that the seed is something powerful and life-giving. Ultimately, the seed will produce a harvest of life-sustaining grain. And Jesus was persistent in making that point. His words were to be heard and obeyed. The message was not simply propaganda, nor simply a series of statements to be affirmed in order to gain admission to the kingdom. The Word itself is powerful, producing the needed radical change. It is the life-giving seed. Isaiah explains that some things in nature just happen inevitably: if you are a patient farmer, you will know that, along with the seed, you need sun, moisture and good soil. Then, in time, there will be a crop. Just as in the natural world, so too in the spiritual world. When God sends his Word, it achieves its purpose. When God speaks, something happens. Nothing can frustrate or divert his Word: it 'will accomplish what I desire and achieve the purpose for which I sent it' (Isaiah 55:11).

So, as we think about our responsibility to respond to the Word, our task is to welcome in that life-changing power: 'Get rid of all moral filth and the evil that is so prevalent, and humbly accept the word planted in you, which can save you' (James 1:21).

Pressing it home

Eric Alexander tells the story of someone describing Robert Murray McCheyne of Dundee: 'He seemed, as his preaching progressed, to advance upon you until he was standing inside your heart, applying the Word of God to all your life.'[4] Have you ever had that experience? The reason why preaching matters is that we are declaring the good news of a gracious God. We long for his Word to comfort the distressed, to strengthen the weak, to confront the self-sufficient, to disturb the complacent, to guide the uncertain, to equip the disciple, to envision the church, to challenge society . . . and so much more. The central need in all such pastoral preaching is to address the affections, to appeal to the heart, as well as to the mind and the will. Congregations are hugely diverse in terms of their needs, and this calls for sensitivity in preaching: 'We have no liberty to preach the word in such a way as to be indifferent to whether anybody is listening, or to whether our audience consists of wooden pews instead of living, breathing persons.'[5]

Faithful exposition will follow where the Bible passage leads, and it will do its work. Our task is to ensure it is clear and plain, focused on the key theme or heartbeat of the passage, drawing out its abiding significance in specific ways that will help our hearers: 'Why is this passage important for me, and what must I do in response?'

Think of Jesus and his word to the rich young ruler. Jesus knew his heart, his motives and his idolatry, and he couldn't have been more direct: 'If you want to be perfect, go, sell your possessions and give to the poor, and you will have treasure in heaven. Then come, follow me' (Matthew 19:21). Paul's preaching was equally uncompromising in its naming of specific sins to be renounced and specific godly qualities to pursue. The New Testament preachers addressed the conscience, through careful explanation addressed to the mind, urging a response to God's grace.

Preaching, then, must apply the truth of Scripture to the speaker and the hearer, with the overriding concern to press the truth home, so that, through the power of the Word and the Spirit, the listener understands and responds.

10

Biblical preaching must depend on God's Spirit

Apparently, it was the habit of the great Baptist preacher, C. H. Spurgeon, every time he mounted the steps of the pulpit at the Metropolitan Tabernacle in London to say quietly under his breath, 'I believe in the Holy Ghost, I believe in the Holy Ghost.'

Even if the story is apocryphal, Spurgeon's ministry affirmed the importance of the Spirit's work: 'Men might be poor and uneducated, their words might be broken and ungrammatical; but if the might of the Spirit attended them, the humblest evangelist would be more successful than the most learned divine or the most eloquent of preachers.'[1]

Depending on the Spirit's presence and empowering is essential in the work of proclaiming God's Word. Whilst we wish to be equipped with the skills to understand Scripture, exploring the best hermeneutical and homiletical techniques, the great danger is that this calling is reduced to a mere technical exercise. But as Eric Alexander has pointed out, preaching is a spiritual exercise: 'It is possible to be homiletic-ally brilliant, verbally fluent, theologically profound, biblically accurate and orthodox, and spiritually useless.'[2]

We need only look at how Jesus, Peter and Paul depended on the Holy Spirit to understand that we too certainly need to do the same! When Jesus was in the Nazareth synagogue, he applied Isaiah 61:1 to himself:

> The Spirit of the Lord is on me,
>> because he has anointed me
>> to proclaim good news to the poor.
> (Luke 4:18)

The apostles 'preached the gospel to you by the Holy Spirit sent from heaven' (1 Peter 1:12). And twice, Paul declares that his preaching was dependent on the Holy Spirit: 'Our gospel came to you not simply with words but also with power, with the Holy Spirit and deep conviction' (1 Thessalonians 1:5), and: 'My message and my preaching were not with wise and persuasive words, but with a demonstration of the Spirit's power, so that your faith might not rest on human wisdom, but on God's power' (1 Corinthians 2:4–5).

This chapter sits within the section concerning 'the congregation and the purpose of preaching', because the Spirit's active work will be as much in the listener as in the speaker. Indeed, for every believer, the Christian life is life in the Spirit.

The Spirit and the Word

One of the strengths of the Keswick movement through its history and around the world has been its commitment to ensure that Spirit and Word are held together. We know that an unfortunate polarization can occur, so much so that some churches might be inappropriately caricatured as centred on the Word but devoid of the Spirit, whilst others might be committed to the Spirit whilst neglecting the Word. But any such divorce of Word and Spirit is impossible because it is unbiblical.

First, *the Spirit inspires the Scriptures*. Peter reminds us that 'no prophecy of Scripture came about by the prophet's own interpretation of things. For prophecy never had its origin in the human will, but prophets, though human, spoke from God as they were carried along by the Holy Spirit' (2 Peter 1:20–21). The biblical writers were moved by the Spirit, 'carried along' just as the wind carries along a sailing ship. The Spirit of God, working through the diverse personalities, contexts and cultures of its human authors, supervised the Scriptures which we now seek to understand, obey and proclaim.

Secondly, *the Spirit illuminates or enlightens the hearers of Scripture*. The Spirit is at work in the hearts and minds of believers, helping us to embrace that Word. Without the work of God's Spirit, we could never understand the word of the gospel. Paul makes it clear in his letter to the Corinthians, having first described how the apostles themselves received the Spirit and spoke in words taught by the Spirit: 'The person without the Spirit does not accept the things that come from the Spirit of God but considers them foolishness, and cannot understand them because they are discerned only through the Spirit . . . But we have the mind of Christ' (1 Corinthians 2:14–16).

Thirdly, *the Spirit equips believers*, and this includes every believer called to proclaim the gospel message and confess Christ's lordship. This is impossible without the Spirit (1 Corinthians 12:3). The gifts to the church, including those who minister the Word, are given by the Spirit, just as he determines (1 Corinthians 12:11). Our abilities both to understand and teach the Scriptures are the work of the Holy Spirit given to believers and the local church.

This is precisely why we need to keep Word and Spirit together. Klaus Bockmuehl has written on this subject in *Listening to the God Who Speaks*, where he reminds us of the work of the Holy Spirit:

> He is 'the teacher within', as the ancient church called him. He brings to us the continuing presence of Christ as mediator, communicator, bridge-builder, 'the go-between' God. The passages in John that deal with the Holy Spirit are full of communication verbs. So the Holy Spirit is the teacher who speaks, rebukes, reminds and guides. In Christian circles, he is far too often represented merely as the enabler, and thus is reduced to a mute 'force' or impersonal agent.[3]

This provides enormous encouragement to all of those who are to exercise a ministry of the Word. When these things are aligned – the Spirit-inspired Scriptures, the Spirit-illumined mind of the believer and the Spirit-equipped teacher – such ministry will be fruitful. And the focus, as we will see in our final chapter, will inevitably be Jesus himself, for the Father gave the Spirit in order to glorify his Son (John 16:14–15).

The Spirit and the preacher

In the same way as the Spirit inspired the biblical writers, and the biblical writers engaged in their task of speaking and writing, so the same inseparable partnership applies to the work of preaching. We are deeply dependent upon the Spirit's presence, but are still called to devote all of our energies to rightly 'dividing the Word' and explaining its meaning and message. Indeed, it is humbling to remember that, if the Spirit inspired the Word, and the Spirit illumines and convicts, then 'ours is only the second sermon; the first and last are those of the Holy Spirit, who first gave his Word and quickens it in the hearts of hearers'.[4]

The marriage of Word and Spirit is seen in the calling and ministry of Ezekiel, from whose example we can learn. Ezekiel was called by the Lord: 'Son of man, stand up on your feet and I will speak to you' (Ezekiel 2:1). Then, in the very next verse, we read, 'As he spoke, the Spirit came into me and raised me to my feet, and I heard him speaking to me.' Sent by that Spirit (verse 3), the Lord called Ezekiel to proclaim his Word, whether or not people would listen (verse 7), and then presented Ezekiel with the Word: 'Then I looked, and I saw a hand stretched out to me. In it was a scroll . . .' (verse 9). And in a memorable image, the Lord said to Ezekiel, '"Son of man, eat what is before you, eat this scroll; then go and speak to the people of Israel." So I opened my mouth, and he gave me the scroll to eat' (Ezekiel 3:1–2).

So much of what we have discussed about the task of preaching is expressed here: the calling from the Lord himself to speak his Word; the empowering presence of the Spirit who helps us to our feet and sends us on that mission; the inevitable challenges of speaking to those who will not receive the Word; and the essential commitment to receive the Word like food from heaven, making it our own. The preacher knows all too well that Word and Spirit belong together.

> *The preacher knows all too well that Word and Spirit belong together.*

Indeed, a former colleague of mine, Chris Wright, sometimes suggested that there are three people in the pulpit when the Word is preached. There is the preacher, opening the Bible with prayer and humility, having done all the work to understand the passage. Then, there is the Holy Spirit who inspired the words and wants to use the preacher's words to speak his message into hearts, minds and wills. And then, there is the original author, the person who, under the Spirit's inspiration, wrote the Bible book. We should imagine him by our side or looking over our shoulder, and ask ourselves whether he would agree that what we are saying was what he meant to say.

The Spirit and the listener

All believers must depend on the Spirit. The Spirit opens our hearts and minds to the truth of the gospel; he brings us new life through that Word; he indwells us, making God's love real to us and pointing us to Christ. And so, as we gather as a congregation, the Spirit is within and among us. All of us must seek his illuminating presence as we listen to the preached Word. We have already seen Paul's testimony to the Thessalonians that, when he brought them the gospel message, it 'came to you not simply with words, but also with power, with the Holy Spirit and deep conviction' (1 Thessalonians 1:5). But in the very next verse, he demonstrated that the Spirit was also at work in the listeners, in the Thessalonians themselves, enabling them to welcome that Word: 'You became imitators of us and of the Lord, for you welcomed the message in the midst of severe suffering with the joy given by the Holy Spirit' (1 Thessalonians 1:6).

So here is what really matters as we gather on Sunday: the Spirit will be at work to convict us of sin, to convince us of God's mercy, to confirm within us God's love, to point us to Jesus himself. Paul prays that believers will grow in their understanding through the work of the Spirit. In the trinitarian prayer of Ephesians 1, notice the significance of the relationship between prayer, the Holy Spirit and our understanding:

I keep asking that the God of our Lord Jesus Christ, the
glorious Father, may give you the Spirit of wisdom and
revelation, so that you may know him better. I pray that the
eyes of your heart may be enlightened in order that you may
know the hope to which he has called you, the riches of his
glorious inheritance in his holy people, and his incomparably
great power for us who believe.
(verses 17–19)

Do we long to know God better? Then listening to God's
Word in this prayerful, reflective mode, seeking the Spirit's
illuminating presence and power, is vital not just for preachers,
but for every believer committed to that highest goal of all.

11

Biblical preaching must proclaim God's grace in Christ

Martin Luther used to describe Scripture as the cradle in which we will find the baby. Its purpose is not to draw attention to itself, but to the person of Jesus. And this is a fitting conclusion to a book on biblical preaching. It underlines why, in the Keswick movement which seeks 'the spiritual renewal of God's people for his mission in the world', the Bible is central. For the Scriptures – Old and New Testaments – point to Jesus Christ. As we have seen, Paul explained his priorities in preaching when defending himself against his critics in Corinth. In 2 Corinthians 4, he stresses that he explained the Word of God clearly (verse 2) and presented Christ faithfully: 'For what we preach is not ourselves, but Jesus Christ as Lord, and ourselves as your servants for Jesus' sake' (verse 5). Christ-centred preaching is the fundamental priority.

The story in Nehemiah 8 demonstrates how the reading of the book of the law exposed the sin of the people – so they wept – but pointed them to the mercy of God – so they rejoiced. Then, in Nehemiah 9, the people confessed their sin, enjoyed God's grace and renewed their commitment to him. Biblical preaching must seek to have the same impact. It must be grace-filled. And for us, standing now in the light of the New Testament, to preach grace, we must preach Christ.

Jim Packer drew some lessons for preachers from the Puritans, one of which was the importance of a Christ-centred orientation: 'The preacher's commission is to declare the whole counsel of God; but the cross is the centre of that counsel, and the Puritans knew that the traveller through the Bible landscape misses his way as soon as he loses sight of the hill of Calvary.'[1]

The central story

Much of this book has focused on the Bible – our conviction about its authority, our confidence in its power and our responsibility for the handling of its message. Those who hold a high view of Scripture are often accused of believing in a distorted trinity of Father, Son and Holy Bible, or are charged with being 'bibliolaters'. But such critics misunderstand why evangelicals pay such careful attention to the Scriptures as the Word of God. Alister McGrath explains, 'Christianity is Christ-centred, not book-centred; if it appears to be book-centred, it is because it is through the words of Scripture that the believer encounters and feeds upon Jesus Christ. Scripture is a means not an end, a channel, rather than what is channelled.[2]

Earlier, we saw how, on the road to Emmaus, Jesus chose not to reveal himself directly to the disciples, but deliberately placed the Scriptures before them, explaining that these pages spoke of him (Luke 24:25–27, 44–49). Of course, we more easily grasp the fact that the New Testament speaks of Jesus Christ – we understand immediately that its writers focus on Christ, for the Scriptures 'are able to make you wise for salvation through faith in Christ Jesus' (2 Timothy 3:14–15). But on the road to Emmaus, Jesus was pointing them back to the Old Testament Scriptures. They too spoke of him. So, the *whole Bible* is given to us for precisely this reason – to bring us into a living relationship with Jesus Christ, the Living Word. The Bible is the Father's testimony to the Son, and we know that he is the focal point of all of Scripture. Jesus frequently made this clear. For example:

'You study the Scriptures diligently because you think that in them you have eternal life. These are the very Scriptures that testify about me.'
(John 5:39)

'If you believed Moses, you would believe me, for he wrote about me.'
(John 5:46)

The scroll of the prophet Isaiah was handed to him. Unrolling it, he found the place where it is written: 'The Spirit of the Lord is on me, because he has anointed me to proclaim good news to the poor. He has sent me to proclaim freedom for the prisoners and recovery of sight for the blind, to set the oppressed free, to proclaim the year of the Lord's favour.' Then he rolled up the scroll, gave it back to the attendant and sat down. The eyes of everyone in the synagogue were fastened on him. He began by saying to them, 'Today this scripture is fulfilled in your hearing.'
(Luke 4:17–21)

And beginning with Moses and all the Prophets, he explained to them what was said in all the Scriptures concerning himself.
(Luke 24:27)

This means that we study and preach the Scriptures with the purpose of knowing Jesus and making him known.

> Any preoccupation with the biblical text which does not lead to a stronger commitment to Jesus Christ, in faith, love, worship and obedience, is seriously perverted. It brings us under the rebuke of Jesus: 'You search the Scriptures, because you think that in them you have eternal life; and it is they that bear witness to me; yet you refuse to come to me (to whom they bear witness) that you may have life.'[3]

Integrity in the preacher and the preaching

The preacher's first concern is that his own life is being transformed – that our 'praying the Word', our understanding and application of Scripture, our experience of the Spirit, should be producing ever-increasing Christlikeness. Our personal concern must be to pursue the maturity to which Paul points: 'Just as you received Christ Jesus as Lord, continue to live your lives in him, rooted and built up in him, strengthened in the faith as you were taught, and overflowing with thankfulness' (Colossians 2:6–7).

This is where preachers must begin, first for their own spiritual health and growth, but also to ensure that their preaching has integrity and authenticity. As Bryan Chapell expresses it,

> Grace-focused ministers recognize the daily repentance that private prayers must include, confess to others the divine aid that grants them the strength for their resolutions, obey God in loving thankfulness for the forgiveness and future Christ supplies, model the humility appropriate to a fellow sinner, express the courage and authority of one confident of the

Savior's provision, exude the joy of salvation by faith alone, reflect the love that claims their souls, and perform their service without any claim of personal merit.[4]

Paul had a wonderfully Christocentric mission statement: 'He is the one we proclaim, admonishing and teaching everyone with all wisdom, so that we may present everyone fully mature in Christ. To this end I strenuously contend with all the energy Christ so powerfully works in me' (Colossians 1:28–29). Significantly, in verse 25, he indicates that preaching Christ means preaching from the whole of Scripture, for his task is 'to present to you the word of God in its fullness'. Preaching Christ does not mean artificially making every verse be 'all about Jesus'. Clearly, many parts of the Bible are not 'about Jesus' in a direct sense, and we should not twist them and force him into them. We need to listen carefully to what every passage is actually saying and what God wants to teach us through it. However, the whole Bible witnesses to Christ, either as a story that leads up to him (in the Old Testament) or as the direct testimony about him (in the New Testament).

In speaking of Christ in all the Scriptures, we must honour the principles of careful exegesis which we have touched on. For those who would like a careful treatment of the topic, I would recommend *Christ-Centered Preaching* by Bryan Chapell,[5] which sets the theme within the wider context of the entire matrix of God's redemptive work. This is to underline what we saw in chapter 3 – that we must understand a Bible passage in its own context, but also in relation to the rest of the Bible. This is not a narrow agenda, but 'the whole will of God', as Paul called it in Acts 20:27, for all of Scripture reveals the plan and purpose of God that is centred on Christ. So, once again, this is our purpose: 'He is the one we proclaim, admonishing and teaching everyone with all wisdom, so that we may

present everyone fully mature in Christ. To this end I strenuously contend with all the energy Christ so powerfully works
in me' (Colossians 1:28–29).

Preaching for change

So, the Bible must be central because, as God's authoritative
Word, it reveals his ways to us. Its message is basic to becoming
what we should be as human beings and as God's new society.
The Scriptures are not for information but for *formation,* as God
shapes us by Word and Spirit, transforming us into our
true being. That true being is the likeness of Jesus Christ
himself. Paul describes the glory of our new-covenant ministry
in precisely these terms. Speaking of the Jewish people in
2 Corinthians 3, he describes how a veil covers their hearts so
that they cannot understand: 'It has not been removed, because
only in Christ is it taken away' (2 Corinthians 3:14). He
continues, 'But whenever anyone turns to the Lord, the veil is
taken away. Now the Lord is the Spirit, and where the Spirit of
the Lord is, there is freedom. And we all, who with unveiled
faces contemplate the Lord's glory, are being transformed into
his image with ever-increasing glory, which comes from the
Lord, who is the Spirit' (2 Corinthians 3:16–18). By the Spirit,
we are becoming more like Jesus himself.

In his final public address, John Stott made this his theme.
It was at the Keswick Convention in 2007, and the subject was
well chosen, not least because it represented the purpose of
Scripture, the purpose of preaching, and God's purpose for
his people through the work of Father, Son and Spirit: 'I want
to share with you where my mind has come to rest as I
approach the end of my pilgrimage on earth and it is – God
wants his people to become like Christ. Christ-likeness is the
will of God for the people of God.'[6]

John Stott not only preached this; he embodied it. A former colleague of his once wrote that Stott's most memorable sermon was without a pulpit, surrounded by mud, with Stott standing on a small piece of carpet, speaking to a handful of people in a dark courtyard in India. His Bible text was John 3:16.

> The words were simple and clear. The tone was compassionate and dignified. The assurance was personal and tender . . .
> The sermon on the carpet was memorable because it was the sermon that was John's life . . . For what still draws me to John more than anything else is the aroma of John's life – a life centred and matured in the love of Jesus Christ that bears fruit to the glory of God.[7]

Wherever preaching happens around the world, in whatever cultural context, in however grand or simple a place, in a cathedral or under a tree, there is no more urgent priority than this. All preaching must be biblical, and biblical preaching will be Christ-centred. So, we return to the prayer for the 1880 Keswick Convention. Why preach the Bible? 'Our prayer was for deep, clear, powerful teaching, which would take hold of the souls of the people, and overwhelm them, and lead them to a full, definite, and all-conquering faith in Jesus.'

There can be nothing more urgent or significant than this. Peter longed that through such preaching, the glory would go to God. He expressed it perfectly:

> If anyone speaks, they should do so as one who speaks the very words of God. If anyone serves, they should do so with the strength God provides, so that in all things God may be praised through Jesus Christ. To him be the glory and the power for ever and ever. Amen.
> (1 Peter 4:11)

Appendix 1

Suggestions for further study and discussion

1. Read Nehemiah 8 and 9, noting the responses and the impact of the reading of God's law on the people. Spend some time working through each paragraph of the remarkable prayer of Nehemiah 9. Try to summarize each section with one sentence that captures the attitude of the people and the Lord's response. Write out the specific encouragements from this prayer that you can take to heart in your own life.

2. There are some powerful illustrations of the dynamic of God's Word in the following passages. How do they strengthen our understanding of the ways in which the Bible works in our lives and is effective in fulfilling God's purposes, not least through biblical preaching?

Psalm 33:4–9
Psalm 119:11, 89, 105, 130
Isaiah 55:11
Jeremiah 23:29
Luke 8:1–15
John 8:32
Acts 12:24
Ephesians 6:17
Colossians 3:16
2 Timothy 2:9
Hebrews 4:12, 13
James 1:18

1 Peter 1:23–25
1 John 2:14

3. Read Paul's encouragements to Timothy in the following passages, and identify what each of the commands represented for Timothy, and then what they represent for preachers who are serving in your context.

1 Timothy 4:11–16
2 Timothy 3:14–17
2 Timothy 4:1–5

4. Look at Colossians 1:28 – 2:7 and 2 Timothy 3:16–17 and discuss how you would summarize the primary purposes of biblical preaching which these passages outline. Then write a series of practical guidelines on how such purposes can be achieved through your own biblical preaching – what needs to change in your approach, style and content? What will this require in terms of preparation? What needs to be emphasized more strongly?

Appendix 2

Worksheet for understanding a Bible passage

A. Understanding a passage in context		
Literature	Author, situation, people	Author's purpose
B. Understanding a passage in detail		
Words, people, repetition, links	Divisions	Main theme
C. Understanding a passage in relation to the whole Bible		

Appendix 3

How to work as a group on a manuscript Bible study

1. Read through the entire text several times.
2. Begin to mark repeated words and phrases or elements that stand out:
   - Notice people (who), places (where), time (when) and events (what).
   - Use the same colour for repeated ideas, or for warnings, commands, descriptions of character, lifestyle, etc.
   - Try to define unclear words or phrases.

3. Begin to explore how the passage fits together:
   - Look for 'laws of composition' – repetition, contrasts, cause and effect, or 'juxtaposition' (the laying of two events or sayings side by side as commenting on each other).
   - Draw arrows to connected themes or ideas.
   - Imagine yourself writing the passage and decide where to put paragraph breaks. What is the flow of thought?

4. Isolate the big themes
   - Highlight what might be key verses, or verses to focus attention on.
   - What are the themes that stand out to you as significant?

5. Keep exploring!
   - Any cross-references that come to mind, or any general observations, can be written in the margins.
   - Issues or ideas that we don't understand should also be noted in the margin.
   - Look for and record answers to the 'what-does-this-mean?' questions.

6. Summarize
   - Try to record the one main theme of the passage – the purpose or the 'big idea'.
   - Try to show how the passage fits together to make this point clear.

7. Apply
   Move from your discovery of the meaning of the text to the key questions of application:
   - What are the issues here for our Christian life, community? Our attitudes? Our discipleship?
   - What have I found personally encouraging/challenging/refreshing?
   - What themes here can be used as a group for – prayer/worship/obedience/action . . . ?

From text to sermon

Bible passage: _____

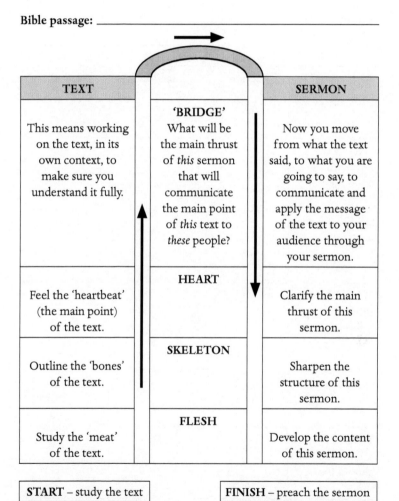

TEXT	'BRIDGE'	SERMON
This means working on the text, in its own context, to make sure you understand it fully.	**'BRIDGE'** What will be the main thrust of *this* sermon that will communicate the main point of *this* text to *these* people?	Now you move from what the text said, to what you are going to say, to communicate and apply the message of the text to your audience through your sermon.
Feel the 'heartbeat' (the main point) of the text.	**HEART**	Clarify the main thrust of this sermon.
Outline the 'bones' of the text.	**SKELETON**	Sharpen the structure of this sermon.
Study the 'meat' of the text.	**FLESH**	Develop the content of this sermon.

START – study the text   **FINISH** – preach the sermon

[Adapted from Ramesh Richard, Scripture sculpture method. Used with permission.]

Appendix 5

Working on the sermon's content

Bible passage: _____

Heartbeat: _____

Verses:	Section 1	Section 2	Section 3
What is the link with the main theme?			
What must I explain?			
What other Bible references should I use?			
What examples could I give?			
What application should I bring?			

Appendix 6

Running a preachers' fellowship group

Around the world, many small groups meet regularly to discuss their preaching, whether they are members of the same church (such as the pastor, the team of lay preachers, the leaders of women's ministry, youth work or home groups), or preachers from different churches in their town. Such fellowship is a great way to encourage us in preparation and sometimes to provide us with helpful feedback.

The PURPOSE of a preachers' group is:

- to meet regularly (perhaps every month or once every two months) to encourage one another in the task of biblical preaching;
- to enjoy fellowship, Bible study and prayer together;
- to share news of what each one is preaching on; share outlines of preaching series; share difficulties and challenges in your Bible preaching ministry; learn from one another;
- to share any resources, books, etc.
- perhaps to set up a small group library of Bible commentaries and study guides that can be borrowed or consulted.

The typical CONTENT of a preachers' group includes:

- *Bible discussion*: choose a short Bible passage and work on it together, establishing the main theme, working on an outline and sharing ideas on how to preach this passage.

- *Asking people to present their outlines*: one or two people bring a passage and their first ideas for a sermon they have to give a week or more after the meeting. The group discusses the passage and outline ideas, bringing new thoughts to help the person (and the whole group) in the preparation of how to preach the passage.
- *Discussing specific issues*: for example, how to plan a preaching programme for the next three months; how to preach from a parable / epistle / minor prophet, etc.; preaching evangelistically; preaching and pastoral ministry; preaching in the context of church worship; how to pray, study and prepare; and much else . . .
- *Developing a small local training programme*: using the preachers' group to cover key issues of preaching training for other lay preachers in our church or town.
- *Praying together* for the preaching ministry in our churches, our own spiritual life, our families and work.

Appendix 7

Evaluating a sermon

Here are some questions by which to assess your own sermon, and perhaps also to distribute to a congregation to enable feedback – not simply for the preacher's benefit, but as a means of helping everyone to appreciate the content and import of a Bible message, while also helping new preachers to strengthen their approach to preparation.

Faithfulness

1. Did the sermon express the main point of the Bible passage that was preached from?
2. Did the sermon stay close to the text that was being preached from and explain what the original author meant?
3. If other Bible texts were referred to, did they throw helpful light on the main text of the sermon, or did they distract from it and confuse people?
4. Was the sermon faithful to the overall message of the biblical faith? In other words, was it balanced and true to the whole of Scripture, or did the preacher misuse the text to push a narrow or unbalanced message that would not be supported by the rest of the Bible?

Relevance

1. How did the preacher build bridges from the world of the biblical text to the world of today?

2. Were any of the illustrations used appropriate to your own context and helpful in explaining the relevance of the text (or, alternatively, inappropriate and irrelevant!)?

3. In what other ways would you have applied this text if you had been preaching it?

Clarity

1. Was the message clear?
2. If so, what methods did the speaker use to make the structure clear?
3. If not, how could the speaker have made it more clear?
4. How did the speaker help you to follow and remember what was said?

Notes

Preface

1. The Keswick lecture was reproduced as a chapter in Christopher J. H. Wright and Jonathan Lamb (eds.), *Understanding and Using the Bible* (SPCK, 2009). I am grateful to SPCK for granting me permission to reproduce some of the material from that title.

Introduction

1. J. I. Packer, 'Why Preach?', in *Honouring the Written Word of God: Collected Shorter Writings of J. I. Packer* (Paternoster Press, 1999), p. 260.

1. Biblical preaching must be centred on God's Word

1. Edmund P. Clowney, *Preaching and Biblical Theology* (Eerdmans, 1961), pp. 54–59.
2. David Day, *A Preaching Workbook* (SPCK, 1998), p. 18.
3. Ibid., p. 21.
4. J. I. Packer, *God Has Spoken* (Hodder & Stoughton, 1979), p. 10.
5. J. R. W. Stott, 'The Paradoxes of Preaching', in Greg Haslam (ed.), *Preach the Word! The Call and Challenge of Preaching Today* (Sovereign World, 2006), pp. 43–44.
6. J. R. W. Stott, *I Believe in Preaching* (Hodder & Stoughton, 1982), p. 126.
7. Quoted in Philip Ryken, *Preach the Word* (Crossway, 2007), p. 202.

8. Haddon Robinson, 'The Relevance of Expository Preaching', in *Preaching to a Shifting Culture* (Baker Books, 2004), p. 80.
9. Christopher Ash, *The Priority of Preaching* (Christian Focus, 2009), pp. 107–122.
10. I realize that 'Native American' is a better description today.
11. Haslam, *Preach the Word!*, p. 250.

2. Biblical preaching must pray God's Word

1. Michael Quicke, *360-Degree Preaching* (Baker Academic/ Paternoster Press, 2003), p. 38.
2. Merrill C. Tenney, *Galatians: The Charter of Christian Liberty* (Eerdmans, 1950), pp. 207–208.
3. For a fuller treatment of this theme, see my chapter on 'Using the Bible Devotionally for Life', in Christopher J. H. Wright and Jonathan Lamb (eds.), *Understanding and Using the Bible* (SPCK, 2009).
4. David Jackman, in Philip Ryken (ed.), *Preach the Word* (Crossway, 2007), p. 13.
5. Eugene H. Peterson, *Eat This Book: A Conversation in the Art of Spiritual Reading* (Hodder & Stoughton, 2006), p. 87.
6. J. R. W. Stott, *I Believe in Preaching* (Hodder & Stoughton, 1982), p. 220.
7. J. I. Packer, *Knowing God* (Hodder & Stoughton, 1973), p. 18.
8. Stott, *I Believe in Preaching*, p. 222.

3. Biblical preaching must understand God's Word

1. Eugene Peterson, *Eat This Book: A Conversation in the Art of Spiritual Reading* (Hodder & Stoughton, 2006), p. 55.
2. Download the reading scheme from http://www.esv.org/ assets/pdfs/rp.one.year.tract.pdf. It is also the basis for the daily readings in D. A. Carson, *For the Love of God* (IVP, 1998).
3. J. B. Priestley, *English Journey* (Penguin, 1977), pp. 106–107.
4. The three titles by Alan Stibbs on handling Scripture have been republished as *The Alan Stibbs Trilogy: Understanding, Expounding & Obeying God's Word* (Authentic Media, 2009).
5. David Day, *A Preaching Workbook* (SPCK, 1998), p. 31.
6. J. R. W. Stott, *Understanding the Bible* (Scripture Union, 2011), pp. 175–195.

Section B: Warm-up

1. H. G. M. Williamson, *Ezra, Nehemiah*, Word Biblical Commentary, vol. 16 (Word Books, 1985), pp. 289, 298.

4. Biblical preaching must be focused

1. Quoted in J. R. W. Stott, *I Believe in Preaching* (Hodder & Stoughton, 1982), p. 226.
2. Bryan Chapell, *Christ-Centered Preaching: Redeeming the Expository Sermon* (Baker Academic, 2005), p. 44.
3. Alan Stibbs, *Understanding, Expounding and Obeying God's Word* (Authentic Media, 2009), p. 101.
4. Ramesh Richard, now developed in *Preparing Expository Sermons: A Seven-Step Method for Biblical Preaching* (Baker Books, 2001).

5. Biblical preaching must be clear

1. David Day, *A Preaching Workbook* (SPCK, 1998), pp. 22–23.
2. There are many suggestions about what makes a good outline, and in making these three points, I am indebted to both Stuart Olyott, *Preaching Pure and Simple* (Bryntirion Press, 2005), ch. 3, and Bryan Chapell, *Christ-Centered Preaching* (Baker Academic, 2005), ch. 6.

6. Biblical preaching must be relevant

1. Darrell W. Johnson, *The Glory of Preaching: Participating in God's Transformation of the World* (IVP Academic, 2009), p. 159.
2. Eugene H. Peterson, *Run with the Horses: The Quest for Life at Its Best* (IVP, 1983), p. 54.
3. Graham Johnston, *Preaching to a Postmodern World: A Guide to Reaching Twenty-First Century Listeners* (IVP, 2001), p. 67.

7. Biblical preaching must be embodied

1. Derek Kidner, *Ezra and Nehemiah*, Tyndale Old Testament Commentaries (IVP, 1979), p. 62.
2. Jonathan Lamb, *Integrity: Leading with God Watching* (IVP, 2006).
3. David Day, *Jeremiah: Speaking for God in a Time of Crisis* (IVP, 1987), p. 89.
4. Colin M. Morris, *The Word and the Words* (Epworth, 1975), pp. 34–35.

5. Eugene H. Peterson, *Under the Predictable Plant: An Exploration in Vocational Holiness* (Eerdmans, 1992), p. 113.
6. Charles Simeon, *Evangelical Preaching*, from the Introduction by John Stott (Multnomah Press, 1986), p. xxix.
7. Quoted in J. I. Packer, *A Quest for Godliness: The Puritan Vision of the Christian Life* (Crossway, 1990), p. 76.

Section C: Warm-up
1. J. I. Packer, *A Passion for Faithfulness: Wisdom from the Book of Nehemiah* (Hodder & Stoughton, 1995), p. 150.
2. J. I. Packer, *God Has Spoken* (Hodder & Stoughton, 1979), p. 10.

8. Biblical preaching must involve the congregation
1. William Philip, 'Concerning Preaching', *PT Media*, Paper No. 1 (2002), p. 16.
2. Quoted by David Jackman, in William Philip (ed.), *The Practical Preacher* (Christian Focus/Proclamation Trust Media, 2002), ch. 3, p. 56.
3. Quoted by Michael Quicke, *360-Degree Preaching* (Baker Academic/Paternoster Press, 2003), p. 44.
4. J. I. Packer, *A Quest for Godliness: The Puritan Vision of the Christian Life* (Crossway, 1990), pp. 281ff.
5. Quicke, *360-Degree Preaching*, p. 196.
6. Christopher Ash, *Listen Up! A Practical Guide to Listening to Sermons* (The Good Book Company, 2009). Another valuable title on this theme is David Day, *Embodying the Word* (SPCK, 2005).

9. Biblical preaching must be applied
1. J. R. W. Stott, in Steve Brady and Harold Rowdon (eds.), *For Such a Time as This: Perspectives on Evangelicalism, Past, Present and Future* (Scripture Union/Evangelical Alliance, 1996), p. 89.
2. Bryan Chapell, *Christ-Centered Preaching* (Baker Academic, 2005), p. 52.
3. Dale Ralph Davies, *The Word Became Fresh: How to Preach from Old Testament Narrative Texts* (Christian Focus Publications, 2006), p. 93.
4. Quoted by Eric J. Alexander, *What Is Biblical Preaching?* (P & R Publishing, 2008), p. 27.
5. J. R. W. Stott, *For Such a Time as This*, p. 89.

10. Biblical preaching must depend on God's Spirit

1. Cited by Robert Lescelius, 'Spurgeon and Revival', *Reformation and Revival*, vol. 3, no. 2 (Spring 1994).
2. Eric J. Alexander, *What Is Biblical Preaching?* (P & R Publishing, 2008), pp. 11–12.
3. Klaus Bockmuehl, *Listening to the God Who Speaks* (Helmers & Howard, 1990).
4. Bryan Chapell, *Christ-Centered Preaching* (Baker Academic, 2005), p. 33.

11. Biblical preaching must proclaim God's grace in Christ

1. J. I. Packer, *The Quest for Godliness* (Crossway, 1990), pp. 281ff.
2. Quoted in Peter Lewis, *The Message of the Living God*, Bible Speaks Today (IVP, 2000), pp. 19–20.
3. J. R. W. Stott, *The Bible: Book for Today* (IVP, 1982), p. 34.
4. Bryan Chapell, *Christ-Centered Preaching* (Baker Academic, 2005), p. 39.
5. Chapell, *Christ-Centered Preaching*.
6. John Stott, *The Last Word: Reflections on a Lifetime of Preaching* (Authentic, 2008), p. 19.
7. Mark Labberton, 'The Sermon on the Carpet', in Chris Wright (ed.), *John Stott: A Portrait by His Friends* (IVP, 2011), pp. 187–192.

KESWICK MINISTRIES

The vision of *Keswick Ministries* is *the spiritual renewal of God's people for his mission in today's world*.

We are committed to the deepening of the spiritual life in individuals and church communities through the careful exposition and application of Scripture, with the following priorities:

Lordship of Christ: to encourage submission to the Lordship of Christ in all areas of personal and corporate living.

Transformation by Word and Spirit: to encourage active obedience to God's Word through a dependency upon the indwelling and fullness of the Holy Spirit for life-transformation and effective living.

Evangelism and mission: to provoke a strong commitment to evangelism and mission in the UK and worldwide.

Whole-life discipleship: to stimulate the discipling and training of people of all ages in godliness, service and sacrificial living, equipping them to participate in the mission of God in every area of life.

Unity and family: to provide a practical demonstration of evangelical unity across denominations and across generations.

Keswick Ministries seeks to achieve its aims by:

- sustaining and developing the three-week summer Convention in Keswick UK, teaching and training Christians of all ages and backgrounds;
- providing training for preachers, leaders and youth and children's workers in different parts of the UK;
- strengthening the network of 'Keswick' events in towns and cities around the UK;
- producing and promoting resources (books, DVDs and downloads, as well as TV and radio programmes) so that Keswick's teaching ministry is brought to a wider audience around the world;
- providing a year-round residential centre in Keswick for the use of church groups and Christian organisations;
- encouraging an international movement by building relationships with the many 'Keswicks' around the world, thereby seeking to strengthen local churches in their life and mission.

For further information, please see our website: www.keswickministries.org or contact our office:

E: info@keswickministries.org   *Tel*: 017687.80075

Mail: Keswick Ministries, Convention Centre, Skiddaw Street, Keswick CA12 4BY, England

The Amazing Cross
Transforming lives today
Jeremy & Elizabeth
McQuoid

ISBN: 978-1-84474-587-6
192 pages, paperback

The cross of Christ is the heartbeat of Christianity. It is a place of pain and horror, wonder and beauty, all at the same time. It is the place where our sin collided gloriously with God's grace.

But do we really understand what the cross is all about? Or are we so caught up in the peripherals of the faith that we have forgotten the core? We need to ask ourselves:

• How deep an impact has the cross made on my personality?
• Do I live in the light of the freedom it has won for me?
• Am I dying to myself every day, so that I can live for Christ?
• Do I face suffering with faith and assurance?
• Can I face death in the light of the hope of the resurrection?

The authors present us with a contemporary challenge to place all of our lives, every thought, word and deed, under the shadow of the amazing cross, and allow that cross to transform us here and now.

'It is an ideal introduction to the heart of the Christian gospel, and a very welcome addition to the Keswick Foundation series.'
Jonathan Lamb

Keswick Study Guides by IVP

The Transforming Trinity
Rediscovering the heart of our faith
Elizabeth McQuoid

These seven studies will help you grow in your understanding of the inexhaustible riches of the Trinity. Find out why the Trinity is central to our beliefs and fundamental to the working out of our faith. Learn to worship the triune God more fully, reflect his image more clearly, and experience his transforming power in your life. Learn what it really means to know the Father, follow the Son, and walk in the Spirit. Because the Trinity is at the heart of Christian faith and life.

'A feast for individuals and Bible study groups.'
Sam Allberry

ISBN: 978-1-84474-906-5 | 80 pages, booklet

Really?
Searching for reality in a confusing world
Elizabeth McQuoid

These seven studies help us go deeper into the truth we are offered in Jesus Christ, and to root our lives in it. Because Jesus offers us himself, a reality that satisfies not only our intellectual curiosity, but also the deepest longings of our hearts. He offers us true security and sure hope for the future. He reshapes our thoughts, our life, our identity and our purpose. Real truth is found in Jesus Christ, and knowing him changes everything.

'Really? is a great resource to explore how the Christian message enables us to live with real confidence in the real world.' Tim Chester

ISBN: 978-1-78359-158-9 | 80 pages, booklet

Available from your local Christian bookshop or **www.thinkivp.com**

also by Jonathan Lamb

Integrity
Leading with God watching
Jonathan Lamb

ISBN: 978-1-84474-160-1
176 pages, paperback

Integrity matters. We expect it, naively perhaps, of leaders in all walks of life. We trust people whose words, character and actions are consistent. But why is integrity so rare? Why does our walk not match our talk?

One of the most pertinent and positive examples of integrity in Scripture is that of the apostle Paul. In 2 Corinthians his passions and frustrations are clear as he offers us an extraordinary insight into the joys and pressures of Christian leadership. His model is no less counter-cultural today than it was in the first century: leading with God watching.

Jonathan Lamb examines key passages and interweaves them with examples from everyday life. Whether in responding to criticism, exercising authority, coping with failure, handling money or struggling with personal weakness, this book is a call to live consistently in the light of gospel priorities. Only then will our lives speak authentically to a sceptical world.

'A powerful challenge.' John Stott

Available from your local Christian bookshop or **www.thinkivp.com**

Inter-Varsity Press

For more information about IVP
and our publications visit
www.ivpbooks.com

Get regular updates at **ivpbooks.com/signup**
Find us on **facebook.com/ivpbooks**
Follow us on **twitter.com/ivpbookcentre**

Inter-Varsity Press, a company limited by guarantee registered in England and Wales, number 05202650. Registered office IVP Bookcentre, Norton Street, Nottingham NG7 3HR, United Kingdom. Registered charity number 1105757.